DAMSONS

Dedicated to the women who made
damson 'plum butter' before me:
Rose Charles Conrad
Jennie Holland Conrad
and my beloved grandmother
Marcella Muri Conrad

THE ENGLISH KITCHEN

DAMSONS

An Ancient Fruit in the Modern Kitchen

SARAH CONRAD GOTHIE

PROSPECT BOOKS

2018

This edition published in 2018 in Great Britain and the USA by
Prospect Books at 26 Parke Road, London, SW13 9NG

British Library Cataloguing in Publication Data:
A catalogue entry for this book is available from the British Library.

ISBN 13: 978-1-909248-58-8

Cover by Jackie Vanderzwaag (jackiedoesdesign.carbonmade.com).

Printed by the Gutenberg Press Ltd., Malta.

TABLE OF CONTENTS

PREFACE

If the growing interest in cooking as a leisure hobby since the 1960s – in gastronomical magazines and on television since the 1980s, and more recently in millennial foodie blogs and photo 'feeds' on social media – has demonstrated anything, it is that the old can easily become new again, including long-forgotten recipes conjured up by medieval court cooks, peasant wives, or our own grandmothers. Foods from the past are perennially being remixed, revived, and re-tasted. I grew up in the United States, where the popularity of damsons has lessened significantly over the past century. Orchards still exist, supplying small-scale vintners and jam producers, and nurseries still sell trees, but fresh damsons and the products made from them are far from mainstream. As a child, I delighted each year in early September when my grandmother, Marcella, would make 'plum butter,' a damson preserve my grandfather treasured from his own childhood. He was born in 1920 in Newry, Pennsylvania, and damson trees had grown in the backyard of his family home. His youngest siblings, Wayne and Betty, recalled years later that their grandmother Rose, whose ancestors had come from Wales, would leave a pot of damsons cooking on her wood-burning stove for hours. It's not been possible to trace the recipe back any further, but I'm proud to be a fifth-generation damson enthusiast.

After my grandfather passed away, my grandmother stopped making damson preserves. About fifteen years later, as an adult living in Ohio, I was able to place a special order for damsons through a local farm market and surprise my family at Christmas with the wonderfully tart spread we so fondly remembered. Americans are accustomed to a variety of plums, but most have never heard of damsons; I always had to explain what they were to people outside my family. On my first visit to the Lake District, I found myself in a place where every person I spoke to knew what a damson was. Every farm shop offered multiple brands of damson jam, as well as chutneys and ketchups (and gin!). In the area of Cumbria formerly known as Westmorland, the fruit that had been an idiosyncrasy of my immediate family was a significant part of the local culinary heritage. I returned home committed to learning more about damson cultivation and use in England, and in that process this book was born.

Though this fruit had always felt unique to my family, my research and explorations have affirmed that it is not. Many continue to grow, consume, and cherish damsons. People all over England are working to preserve the ancient plums that have fed their forebears since pre-Christian times. From the Westmorland Damson Association in Cumbria to the Ludlow Marches Slow Food group in Shropshire, present-day enthusiasts are putting on damson fairs, walks, dinners, and talks. Community orchards are being tidied up and a new generation of trees planted. In England, the damson is thriving: not at the pace of its nineteenth century commercial heyday, but on a quieter, more sentimental scale.

When I asked those who already love damsons what they thought would help the fruit find its place in modern kitchens, I received a range of answers: appeal to people who have a genuine interest in foraged or home-grown foods; appeal to chefs who are willing to do the work to bring an unfamiliar ingredient to their patrons' plates; or appeal to Mary Berry to endorse the fruit. My solution is to offer new ways for enthusiasts to enjoy damsons, and to entice newcomers to try them. Throughout the process of writing this book, I've come to believe that, if people unfamiliar with damsons could only taste them, properly prepared, they would require no further encouragement. John Ruskin, who retired to the Lake District and probably consumed his fair share of damsons, writes of the author who 'has something to say which [s]he perceives to be true and useful, or helpfully beautiful'. The truest and most useful thing I have to say is this: damsons are delicious. Give them a try.

SCG

INTRODUCTION

D amsons brighten crumbles, enliven cakes, add lustre to jellies and glisten in gins. They are at home in jars, preserved as jams, sauces and pastes. In all uses, they lend a distinctive and enticing flavour. H.V. Taylor writes, in *The Plums of England*, 'Damsons have a dryness, sweetness, spiciness and bitterness found neither in their near relations, […] nor in any other class of plums.'[1] The damson is a versatile fruit that has been present in the human diet for millennia. Unlike sweet-fleshed, mainstream plums that are the exact size of our palms, and savoured as the juice streams down our chins, damsons are petite and astringent. Damsons have been described as 'everything twenty-first century fruit is not: small, sour and demanding'.[2]

About the size of a large grape, damsons grow robustly in cultivated orchards and in the wild, often thriving in-between as a hedgerow plant. Regardless of milieu, damsons remind us of the seasonal cycle: damson blossoms signal the arrival of spring, and their fruits the onset of autumn. The damson's use in commercial jam-making has fallen sharply since the 1950s: the labour required to collect many small damsons from brittle branches, easy access to a plethora of alternative imported fruits, and a general decline in jam consumption, have caused damsons to fade into the background of rural hedgerows and garden corners. Many people, however, still stand by U.P. Hedrick's assertion, made over a century ago: 'The common Damson, the Damson of the ancients, probably little changed since before Christ's time, is still worthy of cultivation, even though a score or more of its offspring are offered to take its place.' Damsons have spread to orchards in the United States, New Zealand, and elsewhere, but it is in England that they are celebrated and perpetuated, with new plantings, culinary innovations, and revivals of traditional uses.

DEFINING THE DAMSON

Damsons reside within the genus *Prunus*, which includes cherries, apricots, peaches, and plums. *Prunus* species share the attribute of a large central seed with a hard endocarp (a stone) and are commonly referred to as stone fruits. The damson's status within *Prunus* has been subject to centuries of debate. Linnaeus listed *insititia* plums (damsons and bullaces) as a *Prunus domestica* (large, sweet plums) subspecies in 1753, reinforcing Swiss botanist Caspar Bauhin's 1623 divisions.[3] Linnaeus had been the first to broaden the genus *Prunus* to include stone fruits such as peaches and cherries; his predecessors, as well as a number of later botanists, such as Augustin de Candolle (1778-1841), maintained *Prunus* as solely for plums.[4] Some botanists have classified *Prunus insititia* as a subspecies of *Prunus domestica*, while others have argued for its status as a separate species.

Debates about how to classify damsons should not be perceived as a predilection to vacillate on the part of taxonomists, but as evidence of how little really separates these species. That these fruits are so similar may seem surprising, since of all the *Prunus* fruits, plums are the most diverse in their sizes, shapes, colours, textures, flavours, and scents.[5] Shifts in the classification of *insititia* plums have been based on archaeological, geographical, and cytological data, as well as on the evaluation of physical characteristics (colour, blossom structure, tree structure, and stones). *Insititia* as a subgroup of *domestica* was championed by some into the twentieth century, but by the twenty-first, the issue seems to be settled in favour of a separate species. *Insititia* are distinguished from large, sweet plums (*P. domestica*) by their smaller size fruits and smaller size trees, their swollen stones, and their solid coloured skins with no intermediate shades.[6] *P. insititia* currently comprises damsons, bullaces, mirabelles,[7] and St. Julien plums (a cultivar used primarily as a rootstock for grafting).[8]

A popular theory for the origins of *P. insititia* from the 1930s through to the late twentieth century was that they formed through the marriage of a *P. cerasifera* (cherry plum) subspecies[9] and *P. spinosa* (sloe). Hybrids of these have been found occurring spontaneously in the Caucasus region and the two species have been crossed in a lab environment with some success. Investigating the theory that *P. cerasifera* (cherry plum) crossed with *P. spinosa* (sloe) to create damsons, Hendrik Woldring conducted breeding tests and examined stones from intermediate forms of sloe, damson, and cherry plums. He found that crosses of black-fruited damsons with shiny, bitter sloes were almost always fertile, unlike crosses involving other *Prunus* species (such as cherry plum), which were often sterile or inviable. Additionally, the close similarities of the damson and sloe's fruits, blossoms, blossom timing, rootsuckers, and especially stones, led him to conclude that our modern-day *Prunus insititia* likely evolved from *spinosa*, without a contribution from *cerasifera*. With the developments in genetic sequencing that have occurred since Woldring conducted his study, future research should expand our understanding of the damson's ancestry.

If the subtle variations of *Prunus* species haven't generated enough confusion, inconsistent naming has bedeviled *insititia* plums. The name 'damson' derives from the fruit's assumed origins near Damascus, Syria (discussed in the next chapter), a place where a variety of plums were known to have grown. Sixteenth- and seventeenth-century texts reference both 'Damascena' and 'damascene' plums, but these plums appear to be neither ancestral to, nor synonymous with, the plums today called damsons. John Gerard, who possessed a collection of over sixty plum cultivars,[10] used the term 'damson' to refer to some *P. domestica* varieties, as evidenced by an illustration in *The Herball* (1597) captioned 'Prunus Domestica: The Damson Tree.'[11] Jacques Daléchamps, in his *Historia generalis plantarum* (1586), describes 'Damascena' as having 'dark skin, pleasant flesh, and a small stone'.[12] 'Pleasant' is not the first word that comes to mind upon tasting a raw damson. John Lawson, a historian who made an inventory of fruits cultivated in North Carolina in 1714, lists 'damsons' as an item separate from 'Damazeen.'

The extensive list of translated names for damsons provided by Alan Davidson gives an indication of the fruit's possible aliases: *prune de damas* (French), *Dämaszenerpflaume* (German), *sustina di Damasco*, or *prugna damaschina* (Italian), *ciruela damascena* (Spanish), kræge, or *damascenerblomme* (Danish), *krikon* (Swedish), *damaskonluumu* (Finnish), *chernosliv* (Russian), *śliwka damaszka* (Polish), *bardaklija*, or *damaška šljiva* (Serbo-Croat), and *damaskine* (Greek). Even here, the French, *damas*, described in the nineteenth century as sweet and pleasant-tasting with free stones,[13] is offered as a name for the damson. U.P. Hedrick asserts that only in England and America can one count on a plum called 'damson' being an *insititia*: 'The European continental countries have an entirely different conception of a Damson. The Germans speak of all common plums as "Damson-like" while the French use the term *"Damas"* indiscriminately.'[14] One may easily encounter a plum marked 'damson' that is not, in fact, a true *Prunus insititia* specimen.

Damson varieties differ only slightly in appearance, and 'all possess the damson flavour, which is easy to recognise, but difficult to define'.[15] Among the best known,[16] we find some propagated from the suckers of exceptional wild specimens, as well as hybridized damsons that combine their desirable traits of hardiness and vigour with traits of a larger, sweeter *domestica* plum, calling into question whether they ought to be called damsons at all.

Shropshire Prune Damson (also known as **Westmorland Damson** and **Cheshire Prune** when growing in those places), is the most widely available and dependable damson. Thought to be a product of wild selection,[17] the Shropshire Prune is noted for its 'firm, sugary, astringent' flesh,[18] and became popular in the eighteenth century.[19] Robert Hogg, in 1860, writes of the Shopshire: 'It is generally preferred for preserving, and of all the other Damsons makes the best jam.'[20] Taylor notes that 'only one – the Shropshire Prune Damson (aka Westmorland Damson, Cheshire Prune) – possesses that full, rich astringent flavour so pleasing to the palate. This kind should be used for preference'.[21] American plum farmer Eliphas Cope writes, 'The Shropshire Damson is of fine size, ripens late, and is a most excellent fruit, and the only hardy Damson plum for field culture'.[22] U.P. Hedrick, author *The Plums of New York* (1911), sings its praises:

> In America, Shropshire is probably the best known of the Damsons, being found not only in nearly all commercial plantations but in the smallest home collections as well. [...] Shropshire is enormously productive, bearing its load of fruit year after year until it is a standard among fruits for productivity and reliability in bearing. [...] The fruit is of very good size and while in no sense a dessert plum may be eaten out of hand with relish when fully ripe or after a light frost – a point worth considering where only Damsons can be grown. It is one of the best of its kind for culinary purposes. This old variety is still to be recommended for both home and market.[23]

The Shropshire prune remains the only damson tree variety readily available from nurseries in the United States, where it is sometimes called 'Blue Damson'.[24]

Crittenden Damson (c. 1820), also known by the names **Farleigh**, or **Cluster**, originated as a wild seedling cultivated by James Crittenden of Farleigh, Kent. The fruit is dark and bears a light blue bloom; as one of its names suggest, it crops heavily, in clusters. According to Hedrick, the 'sour, sprightly' Crittenden 'ranks high among the Damsons in England but in America it is not a great favorite; just why is hard to say. It is likely that it fails in some tree-character, for, with the exception of being a little too tart, the fruit has few faults'.[25] Elsewhere, Crittenden is characterized as producing small fruits generally inferior to other varieties[26] and it is not considered as richly flavoured as the prune damsons.[27]

Bradley's King (c. 1880) from Nottinghamshire[28] bears larger than average fruit, more reddish in colour than typical damsons, with a light blue bloom.[29] One writer describes its flesh as 'firm, meaty, juicy, pleasantly tart',[30] while another characterizes it as 'almost mealy, sugary, and with little of the bitterness so common to damsons'.[31] This variety was found by the Campden Station to be 'rather weak in flavour' when canned.[32]

Merryweather Damson (c. 1907) is likely a hybrid between a true damson and a *P. domestica* variety, cultivated by Merryweather & Sons nurseries, Southwell, Nottinghamshire.[33] A large damson with distinguishable low, spreading tree profile,[34] Merryweather fruits are 'deep hyacinth-blue with a heavy bloom of lighter blue.'[35] Merryweather has won an award of merit from the Royal Horticultural Society.

Frogmore Damson (c.1870) is thought to have originated at the Royal Gardens at Frogmore. 'Frogmore may be considered among the best of the Damsons in quality for the culinary purposes to which this fruit is commonly put. The flesh is tender, sweet and good, but adheres rather too tightly to the stone.'[36]

French Damson is also suspected to be a damson-domestica hybrid due to the large size of its fruit and tree, and the fact that its large stones are sometimes free instead of clinging. Hedrick proposes that the specimens growing in New York may be synonymous with the plum known as Prune Petit Damas Violet. They ripen later than in Shropshire.[37]

White Damson (c. 1629) is not truly white, but a shade of yellowish green. It was first referenced in the United States in 1806. U.P. Hedrick deems it 'chiefly of historic interest,' and suggests that it may be better classified as a Mirabelle, a French plum 'seldom seen in England'.[38] Shoemaker deems the white damson 'unattractive in appearance because of its mottled greenish-yellow color'.[39]

What about Bullaces?

Bullaces are typically classified as a wild form of damson bearing a smaller, rounder fruit than cultivated damson varieties, though not as small as sloes. Bullaces may be 'black' (purple/blue) or 'white' (yellow/green). Bullaces have been described as 'closely allied' to damsons, since 'the trees, blossoms and leaves seem identical, and on botanical grounds any discrimination would appear arbitrary'. H.V. Taylor finds the distinction between damsons and bullaces unworthy of consideration, and dismisses the issue: 'as these groups are relatively unimportant, no steps have been taken to settle matters'.[40]

The oldest known English cookery text, *The Forme of Cury* (1390), contains a recipe for Erbowle, a pudding made with 'bolas,' which is a medieval spelling of bullace (provoking curiosity about the naming of the Shropshire village called Great Bolas). In this recipe, bullaces are cooked in wine, seasoned with a strong spice mix, thickened with rice flour, and served with a scattering of candied anise seeds. (Further discussion of Erbowle can be found in the chilled desserts chapter.) In 1548, William Turner describes wild and cultivated bullaces in his *Names of Herbes*:

> Ther ar divers kyndes of wilde plumbes and plum trees. Wherof I knoe two severall kyndes at the leste. The one is called the bulles tre or the bullester tre / and the other is called the slo tre or the blak thorn tre. The bulles tre is of two sortes / the one is removed in the gardines / and groweth to the bygnes of a good plum tre. The other groweth in hedges / but it never groweth in to y bygnes of any grete tre / but abideth betwene the lygnes of a tree and a great bushe. I never saw in all my lyfe more plenty of thys sorte of bulles trees / then in Somersetshire.[41]

A Book of Fruits and Flowers (1653) provides a recipe 'To Preserve Bullasses as green as grasse' in which the bullaces are prepared in a syrup much like nineteenth-century damson preserves are:

> Take your Bullasses, as new gathered as you can, wipe them
> with a cloath, and prick them with a knife, and quaddle them
> in two watters, close covered, then take a pound of Clarified
> sugar, and a pint of Apple water, boyle them well together
> (keeping them well scummed) unto a Syrupe, and when your
> Bullasses are well dript from the water, put them into the
> Syrupe, and warm them three or four times at the least, at the
> last warming take them up, and set them a dropping from the
> Syrupe, and boyle the Syrupe a little by it selfe, till it come to
> a jelly, and then between hot and cold put them up to keep
> for all the year.[42]

John Abercrombie comments that the bullace, 'if fully ripe,
eats with an agreeable tart relish' and lauds its late maturation and
suitability for tarts, pies, and preserves.[43] Foragers are fond of bullaces,
which they encounter as small trees or bushes growing in hedgerows.
Bullaces fruit heavier and later in the season than damsons (typically
in October/November), making them useful once fresh damsons are
finished. Spellings and names for bullaces vary by period and region,
and include bolas, bullis, bulloes, bullies, bullum, bullison, scad, and
wild damson.

The four varieties of bullaces are black, white, Shepherd's, and
Langley. Black bullaces are the most common; they are indeed black
in colour, with a purple bloom and firm, sour flesh.[44] The Fruit and
Vegetable Preservation Research Station at Campden found that the
black bullace 'made an attractive pack, but was lacking in flavour'.[45]
Sometimes encountered in East Anglia, white bullaces come to
ripeness in late October and are actually chartreuse with a 'thick
creamy bloom'[46] that may be 'mottled with red' on the side facing
the sun.[47] Shepherd's bullace is larger than black and white varieties,
with a green/gold skin. Langley is not a true bullace at all, rather it
is likely the product of a cross between the Early Orleans plum and
the Farleigh damson that occurred at the nursery of horticulturalist

Harry Veitch in Langley, Berkshire, circa 1902. Despite the 'straggly'[48] appearance of its tree, Langley produces a medium to large, late, damson-like fruit. Taylor deems it the finest of the bullaces, 'if it can be so called'.[49]

Whether damsons and bullaces can be used interchangeably is difficult to say. One finds recipes for bullace puddings, gins, and pastes, which are also common uses for damsons. Some recipes explicitly indicate that bullaces may be used in place of damsons. Though they possess similarities, damsons have a more distinctive, and some say 'better', flavour. Damson enthusiasts describe bullaces as damson-like, but 'murkier', more mealy, less rich, and less sweet. While bullaces growing in hedgerows along public footpaths have the advantage of being 'free' food, recipes for damsons outnumber recipes for bullaces by far, likely due to the damson's superior flavour and texture. People in the past would have used fruit such as they could find, but if one is in the position of having a choice, a Westmorland damson from the Lyth Valley, or a Shropshire Prune damson, should always be chosen over a bullace.

Morphology of a Damson

The Flesh

Damson flesh is firm and yellow-green when raw, mellowing to a golden hue when cooked. When damsons are simmering unstirred in a pan, there is a moment when the skins have split and the bright flesh is just barely tinted with the burgundy colour released from the skins, when the flesh takes on a peachy blush. It is possible to peel standard 'black' damsons prior to cooking to achieve a golden pulp or jam, and I have seen it done as a novel garnish for a slice of damson tart, but I can think of more worthy uses of one's time.

Damson flesh has 'a fine spicy taste'[50] that is 'rather austere till highly ripened'.[51] Mrs Beeton has complimentary things to say about the damson. In Beeton's *Book of Household Management* (1861) she states:

Whether for jam, jelly, pie, pudding, water, ice, wine, dried fruit or preserved, the damson, or damascene (for it was originally brought from Damascus, whence its name), is invaluable. It combines sugary and acid qualities in happy proportions, when full ripe. [...] Amongst the list of the best sorts of baking plums, the damson stands first, not only on account of the abundance of its juice, but also on account of its soon softening. Because of the roughness of its flavour, it requires a large quantity of sugar.

This 'roughness' means damsons are an unpopular fruit for eating out of hand; they 'possess a delightful astringent flavour – but this is too pronounced, until the damsons have been cooked, to give enjoyment'.[52] The high pectin content of the flesh makes damsons ideal for producing jams and the stiff damson paste called 'cheese'. Adding sugar enhances palatability; however, even sweetened, their assertive sharpness complements rich ingredients like butter, cream, cheese, and fatty cuts of meat, and pairs well with flavours of citrus, spices, vanilla, chocolate, berries and other stone fruits.

Raw damsons possess the driest flesh of the plums, coming in at 69.8% water (as a point of comparison, raw Victoria plums contain 79.1%, with other types of plums ranking over 70%),[53] which is why water is often added at the start of cooking, before the fruit's juices are released. Damsons contain 8.6% sugars, a moderate amount compared to sweeter dessert plums. Damsons possess 267 mg of potassium per 100 grams – not quite as high as greengages at 290 mg, but significantly higher than Victorias at 177. The same quantity of banana, a fruit famous for its potassium content, yields 358 mg. Potassium derived from diet is essential to heart and digestive functions...yet another reason to eat more damsons!

The Skin

Damson skins vary within a narrow range of blue-black, though 'white' (yellowish) varieties exist. Damsons start out green as small tender fruitlets that blend with the foliage; their colour doesn't deepen until their terminal size has been reached. A purple phase is followed by the characteristic indigo blue with a smudgy light blue 'bloom', a translucent finish on the fruit's surface that may fade when rubbed but does not wash off. True damsons are black or white; intermediate shades do not occur. The damson's suture line, the indented crease found on one side of most *Prunus* fruits, is less distinct than in other plums.

The damson's blue-black skin turns a deep maroon colour when cooked. The skins soften along with the flesh (at a slower rate, of course) for consumption in preserves or jams. In other preparations, they are rubbed through a sieve to meld with cooked pulp. The jewel-like magenta of cooked damsons continues to deepen in colour the longer the fruit is cooked. Highly condensed damson cheeses may appear dark purple.

One frequently encounters tales, orally and in print, of damsons being used to dye a range of consumer goods, including carpets, uniforms, gloves, and hats. In the market towns of Kendal and Market Drayton, damsons were sold in massive quantities, shipped away by train and lorry for industrial purposes. We know that some went to jam factories, yet, in every place where damsons were grown on a large scale, one hears claims that they were also sold for use in the dyeing of textiles. Stories that damsons were shipped off to dye Lancashire cotton or Ludlow gloves are vigorously promulgated, but never corroborated. Brian Stephens, in a report for English Nature, sought to verify the rumours and found no firm evidence of the commercial use of damsons for dyeing. The Guild of Dyers and Colourists had no records of dyeing with damsons, and experts at the Kidderminster Carpet Museum and the Walsall Leather Museum could find no instance of damsons being used in either industry. Stephens concludes: 'On a small scale, in season, with a local supply, damsons may well have been used for dyeing. The present opinion is that industrially it did not happen, and fairly certainly not after 1856.' The advent of synthetic dyes in 1856 would seem evidence enough to dispel the notion that damsons lent colour to Royal Air Force uniforms in wartime. The persistence of these anecdotes may be attributed to feelings of pride that a local product made an important military contribution. Or, it may be the case that documentation of these industries using damsons has yet to come to light.

From a practical perspective, picking damsons is a labour intensive job, and many, many fruits would be required for such a large industry as that of dyeing. Most condemning to the rumours, however, is the fact that damsons don't make a great dye. Jenny Dean, author of several books on natural textile dyeing, conducted experiments to determine the fitness of damsons for dyes. Dean used damson skins to dye wool, silk, cotton and linen with an alum mordant, in an unmodified sample and with four modifiers (acid, alkaline, copper, and iron). The resulting array of pastel fibres were underwhelmingly pale and not likely to be colourfast. In general, dyes made from red and purple fruits yield weak colours that fade quickly. While plum-coloured goods from tunics to yarn to eyeshadow may bear the colour name 'damson,' none of these products actually derives its colour from the fruit.

The Blossom

Compact, densely clustered damson blossoms of creamy white herald the arrival of springtime, evoking feelings of optimism and anticipation. Sue Clifford and Angela King muse in *England in Particular*, 'Depending on your eye the damson makes a scrawny shrub or a tree of Japanese elegance, unpredictable in its leanings, which for a brief moment in spring flowers white and frothy, [...] turning hedgerows into cappuccino.' In the kitchen, damson blossom makes an attractive edible garnish for springtime salads, puddings, and cocktails.

Five petals is typical, but some varieties (such as Crittenden) may have more, or even double petals.[54] Damson blossoms differ from *domestica* plum blossoms, possessing a bare, rather than fuzzy, pistil and calyx-tube, and, on average, twenty-five stamens instead of thirty.[55] Because damsons blossom early, it's possible for an entire year's crop to be lost to a late frost. Interestingly, the blossoms are quite cold-hardy; it's when the sun thaws a blossom too fast that damage occurs.[56] The blossom's task is to attract pollinators; once pollination is complete, the petals are shed and the show is over.

Blossoms can attract tourists as well. A 1938 editorial in the *Westmorland Gazette* suggested that tourists might be enticed to view the Lyth Valley blossoms and 'take interest in the fruit,'[57] but the *Gazette* had begun printing photographs of damson blossoms as early as 1911. From the 1930s to the 1950s, the newspaper featured photographs by local documentarian of country life Joseph Hardman,[58] whose images of Lyth Valley damson blossoms were reproduced nationally. In the damson's boom years, tourists made springtime outings on charabancs, the horse-drawn precursor to the motor coach, to admire the floriferous orchards and hedgerows. Blossom peepers today may follow in their footsteps by attending the annual Damson Day fair hosted by the Westmorland Damson Association, held almost every April.

The Stone

Like all 'stone' fruits, damsons contain a hard, central seed enclosing a soft inner kernel. Some damson jam and cheese recipes suggest cracking a few stones and adding the kernels to enhance the flavour, with good reason: the kernels (aka *noyaux*) smell like marzipan. If you have the time and the inclination, you can make an outstanding almond extract by soaking damson kernels in vodka for several months. After rubbing cooked damsons through a sieve to make purée, rinse any lingering pulp off the stones, place them on a cutting board or sturdy work surface, and lightly bash each stone with a hammer to reveal its translucent white kernel.[59] Stone fruit kernels contain amygdalin, a compound that converts to hydrogen cyanide during digestion. Consumed cooked, or raw in small quantities, however, the kernels present no threat.

Because damsons are a 'clingstone' fruit, cutting the flesh from the stones can be a time-consuming job. A full third of a small damson's real estate can consist of its stone. The first time my mother and I removed stones from two pecks (about 13 kilos) in one morning, we determined it to be the work of more patient people than us, possibly monks. Catherine Moran, a former artisan producer of damson crème brûlée in Shropshire, partially freezes her damsons, then uses a cherry stoning device to push the stones out while keeping the fruit mostly intact. Fortunately, in many recipes, the stones are left in during cooking and sieved out later. Raw damson juice oxidizes to a dull brown on fingernails and tea towels, so when it is necessary to stone damsons by hand, you may wish to wear protective gloves.

When the fruit has been processed whole (as for preserves and pickled damsons), remember to warn guests to chew with caution to avoid a cracked tooth, or worse. A 1915 medical journal recounts the plight of a four-year-old boy who inhaled a damson stone while eating jam. Following respiratory arrest, tracheotomy, and bronchoscopy, the stone's location in his left bronchus was discovered and it was extracted with forceps. More recently, a dissatisfied customer wrote to *The Sunday Times* to report that the proprietor of a Shropshire café was unapologetic when notified that a single slice of their damson pie contained sixty-three stones.[60] The child made a rapid recovery and the unfortunate diner survived, but such drama ought to be avoided if at all possible.

Lest we go too far in cursing the damson for its tenaciously clinging endocarp, let us consider the stone's finer attributes. Black varieties of damsons are somewhat special in that, if self-fertilized, they will grow 'true to seed'.[61] Unlike an apple, whose seeds will produce genetically different and potentially inferior offspring (inferior for culinary uses, that is), a sown black damson stone will sprout a tree very much like its parent.[62] Trees grown from seed may exhibit increased spinescence (the presence of spines), giving them a somewhat 'wilder' appearance, especially in their early years.[63] The tendency of black damson stones to produce similar offspring is one of the reasons the damson has changed so little over thousands of years: 'The millennia-long unaltered stone morphology would lead one to consider this black-fruited plum to be (one of) the elementary wild form(s) of *insititia*, even though it is now maintained by cultivation.'[64] This is only true of black damsons. Stones from 'white' or reddish damsons are usually sterile, or produce inviable sprouts, because they are the product of damsons crossed with *domestica* plums.

Prunus stones are the most reliable clue to species, and even subspecies, identification, being consistent in features such as size, length, width, and shape, as well as surface grooves and indentations.[65] Much of what we know about damson distribution and consumption in the past has been deduced from stones found in latrines and garbage pits. Let us reflect fondly on the glimpses these stones offer into our culinary history the next time we bite down on one, or spend hours trimming, skimming, or sieving to remove them.

∗

Damsons have been growing in England since the island's earliest recorded history. Whether foraged or cultivated, they have been a familiar part of the landscape, and have starred in a range of traditional recipes. For people in damson-growing areas in Shropshire and Cumbria, damsons may seem 'fundamental,'[66] an unassuming part of life and landscape. Henry Mackley, proprietor of a speciality food store in Ludlow, says that for him damsons are simply a fact of life: 'They exist in the same way that blackberries exist and it's just one of the things that you pick as you go for a walk, one of the very few wild ingredients that one knows how to pick and what to pick without being poisoned.'[67] Inhabitants of urban areas may recognize damsons as a type of plum, but may have never picked, cooked, or even tasted them. Those who recall the deprivation of the war years may have mixed feelings about the fruit; one person recounted her memories of her mother making large quantities of jam from local damson trees that continued to flourish in ignorance of international events, as they had always done, and so nourished the nation in its time of need. In the end, she and her brother hated the fruit: 'We would have loved to have strawberry or raspberry jam instead. The everyday jam was the damson.' With damsons, as with anything, one can have too much of a good thing.

Much changed in the post-war years. The 1944 Fruit-Tree Census showed that 10% of the six million plum trees grown commercially at the time were damsons.[68] Almost sixty years later, damsons represented only 3% of all plums grown in the UK.[69] (As of 2003, damsons were no longer tallied as a separate category.) Though these statistics are estimates that may not align precisely, and the status of damsons in hedgerows is unquantified, the numbers are startling: a figure of more than half a million damson trees less than a hundred years ago has been reduced to an estimated 12,500 trees today.[70]

The next chapter recounts the history of damson cultivation and consumption, with special emphasis on England and the ongoing effort to revive interest in the fruit. After a short section on growing, buying, and storing damsons, the remaining chapters present a collection of damson recipes old and new. I hope you will be inspired to welcome the dazzling colour and inimitable flavour of the ancient damson into your kitchen.

DAMSONS IN ENGLAND

The name 'damson' derives from the fruit's supposed origins near Damascus, Syria, where plums were grown in ancient times and where plums have continued to be cultivated in less arid, coastal areas.[1] Damsons, as well as apricots, cherries, and other plum varieties, are thought to have travelled to the Mediterranean via campaigns led by Alexander the Great (356-323 BCE).[2] Virgil, Horace, Ovid, and Columella all wrote about plums,[3] with Pliny the Elder (23-79) describing the damson as having come from Damascus, but bearing less flesh when grown in Italy.[4] Elite Romans were known to grow a wide variety of fruits as a hobby,[5] but it is thought that most plums cultivated by the Romans were planted in their more northerly territories, which included modern-day Germany and Croatia.[6] The Romans developed methods for orchard management, including grafting techniques to reproduce trees from cuttings.[7] Predictably, damson stones number among the *Prunus* remains found at Roman military camps in Germany and Austria.

There is archaeobotanical evidence, however, that damsons were growing in Europe well before the Romans. Garbage pits excavated at Bronze Age colonies in Switzerland and Germany contained damson stones. Damson stones recovered near Ulm, Germany date to 4060-3956 BCE, and a 6,000 year old damson stone found at Bedburg, Germany, likely came from a Late Neolithic orchard, since wild damsons are not known to have grown in that place during that period.[8] These early stones have provoked disagreement about whether *Prunus insititia* was brought to Europe by Neolithic farmers, or whether it 'could have predated agriculture, and should be regarded as an indigenous element in central Europe'.[9]

In England, the most ancient evidence of *Prunus* is five Middle Pleistocene sloe (*P. spinosa*) fossils found in East Anglian interglacial deposits. Sloe remains from the Middle Bronze, Bronze, and Iron Ages have been found near Glastonbury, and Bronze Age *Prunus* pollen assumed to be sloe was unearthed near Stonehenge. The oldest damson stones in England date to the Late Iron Age and were found at Silchester and Maiden Castle, Dorset. Charcoal remains of Roman period bullaces have been uncovered at Silchester, and of Anglo-Saxon period bullaces at Hungate, Yorkshire.[10] Melitta Weiss Adamson[11] pinpoints 1204 as a year when participants in the Fourth Crusade carried damson trees from Damascus to Europe, but the presence of earlier damson stones proves that damsons were already established in Europe by that time.

Damson stones dating to the Middle Ages have been found across England, Central Europe, and into Scandinavia. While some monasteries cultivated plums, and monastic orchards of the 1200s-1300s may have included damsons (as well as bullaces, mulberries, and quinces),[12] most people of the time would have consumed wild, foraged bullaces and sloes, rather than cultivated fruits.[13] It is not possible to know the role of wild foods in medieval diets, or at what point a wild food source may have shifted into cultivation, but 'in times of dearth, when nothing else was available, the countryside might supply haws, hips, sloes and crab apples' (and bullaces) to abate hunger.[14] Sour plums in the Middle Ages may have been made into verjuice, an acidic component of various sauces (similar to vinegar) that was typically made with unripe grapes or crabapples.[15] Sugar, originally used as a medicine and a spice, arrived in Britain via trade routes through Damascus and northern Italy in the thirteenth century.[16] As techniques for processing and refining sugarcane developed, preservation of ripe fruits as preserves became an option for those who could afford it.[17]

Recovered stones are a tremendous aid to the effort to trace the origins of damsons, but the particularities of how they were grown, prepared, and consumed, and how ancient people felt about the fruit, are impossible to discern. In writing from the sixteenth century onward, we begin to see more detailed descriptions of the uses made of damsons and other plums. Peter Treveris praised damsons as a digestive aid in his *Grete Herball* (1526), saying:

> Plomes be colde and moyst / there be two sortes of them / blacke and reed. The blackes be somewhat harde and amonge them the best be those y be called damaske plommes or damassons. They ought to be gaded when they be rype / If they wyll kepe them must cleve and dewe they with vyneygre / so they may be kep in a vessell of wood. But when they be cloven they must be dryed 15 days in the sonne / and then put in syrope. They have vertue to smothe and polyshe y bowelles.[18]

Leonard Mascall, who was, appropriately enough, from Plumstead in Kent, and the author of *A Booke of the Arte and maner howe to plant and graffe all sortes of trees, howe to set stones, and sowe Pepines to make wylde trees to graffe on* (1569, later ed. 1575), preferred damsons to other plums and advised drying the fruit to preserve it.[19] *A Proper Newe Booke of Cokerye* (1575) and *The Good Huswifes Jewell* (1596) both offer recipes for damson tarts.

The rapid influx of new varieties of fruits and vegetables to England in the sixteenth and seventeenth centuries led to 'a new curiosity' and new modes of food preparation and storage.[20] Just as damsons themselves have not changed over time, the methods for preserving plums and damsons in this period remain familiar today: cooking, sieving, and adding sugar to make jams and pastes (the term damson cheese was not yet common). Cooked, strained fruit pulp, spread onto a dish and dried in the sun, could be used 'to cool the stomach in fevers'.[21] Preservation of fruit is covered at length in seventeenth-century cookery books addressed to the lady of the house, who managed the making of preserves and cordial-waters. Damsons are well-represented in Sir Hugh Plat's *Delightes for Ladies* (1609), which includes a damson conserve made with wine or rosewater, a marmalade of damsons, and 'damson pulpe kept all the yeare'. John Murrell, in *A Delightfull Daily Exercise for Ladies and Gentlewomen* (1621), offers instruction for damson 'pastes, preserves, suckets, marmelates, tartstuffes […] and many other things never before in print'.[22] Damson sweetmeats feature in an elaborate list of refreshments purchased from a London confectioner for the lying-in of the mistress of the Shuttleworth household, Gawthorpe, West Yorkshire, in 1617. These were served to visitors celebrating the birth, alongside aniseed and caraway comfits, sweet biscuits, and other preserved fruits.[23] A latrine used by Royalists at Dudley Castle during the Civil War (1642-1647) contained damson, bullace and sloe stones, suggesting that primitive plum varieties were 'valued for their own sake', despite the availability of larger, cultivated *domestica* plums.[24]

✳

In the nineteenth century, developments in transportation infrastructure permitted damsons to travel quickly from rural areas to urban markets. Lyth Valley damsons journeyed by canal from Hincaster to Preston; in 1870 the *Westmorland Gazette* reported baskets containing 'chiefly damsons from the Flyde' stretching on for nearly a mile in Preston, priced at 1s 1d to 1s 6d per quart.[25] Railway improvements between 1847 and 1876 meant damsons from the Lyth and Winster valleys could arrive in Lancashire and Yorkshire within 24 hours.[26] During this time of railway expansion, damsons also got a boost from the falling price of sugar and the invention of heat-processing to preserve foods on a commercial scale. This technique had its origins in the earlier part of the century, when the Frenchman Nicolas Appert, the inventor of airtight food preservation, began experimenting with heat-processing methods in the hope of winning a contest seeking new ways to preserve the food that travelled with Napoleon's armies. It took fourteen years for him to develop his method of sterilization and sealing. He published a book on his work in 1811 and won the prize of 12,000 francs, with which he opened the world's first cannery.[27a] The ability to safely seal food set the stage for large-scale commercial jam-making, and, for a while, plums of all kinds played a starring role.

In the late nineteenth century, massive plum orchards produced tons of fruit for affordable, wholesome plum jam. From the consumer's perspective, 'variation could be obtained by choosing a different colour week by week, [...] plum jam can be green, pale red, dark red, according to the variety of plum used'. [27b] During this period, 'jam boilers' would buy damsons in bulk direct from Westmorland growers as well as from middleman buyers, in some cases before the fruit had been harvested.[28] Lord Crawford addressed the House of Lords in 1918 on this important pantry staple, saying, 'The needs of the country in the matter of jam are approximately known and they far exceed the supplies at present in sight.' His remarks, reprinted in the *Westmorland Gazette*, go on to describe the efforts of fruit growers in twenty-one counties to 'bring every possible pound of fruit available into the licensed jam factories'.[29]

By the 1920s, however, plum jam had fallen from favour. Consumers wanted soft fruit jams and once the technology existed to import Balkan and Dutch strawberries preserved in a sulphur dioxide solution, 'the quantity of plum jam used had shrunk to insignificance'.[30] In the first forty years of the twentieth century, use of plums for jams dropped from over 50,000 tons to less than 7,000 tons. The plum's fortune would shift again during the Second World War, when sulphited (preserved) soft fruits from the Balkans and the Netherlands were cut off: 'The British public were thrown back on plum jam once again, the demand rising so rapidly that by 1942 or '43 between 40,000 tons and 50,000 tons per year were needed for this purpose.'[31] After the war, the popularity of plums faded once again. The number of plum trees in the UK has been steadily declining since the 1950s.

Despite this commercial decline of plums, damsons have persisted. Wild and cultivated trees contribute to the characteristic appearance of damson-rich Westmorland and Shropshire, where generations have admired the springtime blossoms and feasted on the bounty of autumn fruits. Over the past twenty years, individuals who recognize the cultural and culinary significance of the damson have made efforts to ensure its continued cultivation. A damson renaissance is underway.

DAMSON-GROWING REGIONS

Damsons and bullaces fare well in a range of situations, and can be found growing in most counties of Great Britain. A few counties, however, are known for damsons: in Cumbria, the Lyth and Winster valleys of the area formerly called Westmorland are famous for damsons, and to the south, they're found in higher proportion in the West Midlands fruit-growing counties of Shropshire, Herefordshire, Worcestershire and Gloucestershire, as well as in Cheshire. Damsons in some cases take the name of the place where they grow: the Westmorland Damson and the Shropshire Prune Damson being the best known. In these two places, the past twenty years have seen a remarkable rallying of support for the damson, honouring its long history in each place and renewing public interest in this ancient fruit.

WESTMORLAND DAMSONS

Gastronomic delights beckon throughout the Lake District, from Cartmel, birthplace of sticky toffee pudding, to the tiny hut in Grasmere rolling out slabs of 'world famous' gingerbread. Morecambe Bay is famous for tiny shrimps packed in buttery pots, and Herdwick lamb graces plates in London's finest restaurants, while Kendal mint cake fuels climbers scaling local fells and those summiting Everest.

Within this region of rich culinary heritage, the Westmorland damson remains a cherished local product. In the Lyth and Winster valleys southwest of Kendal, green fields latticed with stone walls and dotted with grazing sheep evoke the setting of a bucolic fairy tale. The valleys are splotched with billowy white blossoms in April, and punctuated with roadside signs advertising fresh damsons in September. The fine limestone soil of these valleys is just right for producing exceptional damsons. The earliest record of damsons being sold at market in Kendal was found in a document kept by a maltster and chair dealer from High Fell End, Witherslack, dated 13 September 1729, but it's likely they were growing there much earlier.

Nineteenth-century records show that every autumn on 'Damson Saturday', carts, crates, and panniers full of damsons lined Highgate in Kendal. The damson's variability is noted in local newspaper accounts of the event. We know that in 1862 damsons were scarce (according to the *Ulverston Mirror*, 'little better than a failure'),[38] and that five years later the Lyth Valley produced a fine crop: 'The crop sometimes differs enormously in quantity and quality with the season, the present year is remarkable for its crop of plums, especially damsons which have hardly ever been known to be so plentiful in the memory of any of the growers. […] the quantities […] which are said to have been got off single trees would read like something almost fabulous.'[39] In 1881, one farmer sold six tons and another, ten tons. 1889 was another excellent year for the damson farmers. During a good year, the fruit can be described as 'dripping' off the tree in heavy, grape-like clusters.[40] The unpredictability of the damson harvest is a likely factor in the fruit's eventual commercial decline, but it adds to the elation damson-lovers feel when a good year comes around.

The apparent peak of damson production for the region came in 1917, with a damson crop estimated to be around nine hundred tons.[41] Mr C.T. Mackintosh, Divisional Inspector for the Board of Agriculture, assessed the Westmorland damson orchards in 1919, two years after the peak production year. Mackintosh believed that the maturity of the trees and the time taken for the fruit to develop (compared to southern varieties) yielded a superior flavour. He judged the approximate age of most of the trees to be sixty years, but criticised their lichen and moss-coated bark (a feature some might find charming).[42] The estimated time of planting – the trees dated back to the 1850s – reflects the role of damsons as a valuable export from the region during that period (coinciding with railway expansion and reduced cost of sugar).

A growers' association was formed in 1938 and established a local canning facility, only to be halted by the war.[43] By 1940, a mere twenty-three years after its peak, the crop estimate had fallen from nine hundred tons to just over two hundred,[44] and in 2006 the Westmorland Damson Association crop estimate was twenty tons. Local historian Desmond Holmes attributes this decline to a reduced demand for jam, increased availability of imported fruits, a reduction in the rural labour force, and a reluctance of growers to collaborate over the long term.[45]

Although twenty-first century numbers can't compare to those of

DAMSONS IN AMERICA

In the late seventeenth century, damsons were reported by John Josselyn to be the sole plum cultivated in colonial-era New England, due in part to the colonists' preference for them, but also due to the practical reason that black damsons tend to grow true to seed, negating the need to transport saplings.[32] Various damson cultivars received a thorough treatment in U.P. Hedrick's encyclopaedic *The Plums of New York* (1911), and in agricultural bulletins and newsletters in the early twentieth century from Ohio, Indiana, Michigan, Missouri, and other states.[33] A 1928 report published by the Ohio Agricultural Experiment Station describes more than twenty damson and bullace varieties, claiming for each some distinguishing characteristic. The author of this report, J.S. Shoemaker, asserts: 'Altho the demand for plums is limited, the value of damsons should not be overlooked. Their characteristic tart, spicy flavor makes them especially desirable for preserves and for other culinary purposes.'[34] A contributor to an issue of *Indiana Farmers' Guide* in 1922 jauntily describes attitudes toward damsons in the Midwestern United States:

a hundred years earlier, the fruit that Clarence Webb, reporting on a 1922 Kendal fruit show, referred to as 'our own peculiar commodity'[46] has been experiencing a renaissance. In 1996, the Westmorland Damson Association (WDA) was formed, following a community meeting organized by Peter Cartmell. The WDA sponsors a springtime Damson Day and maintains a website promoting damsons in the region. The association has produced a map of some forty local farms where damsons are still grown, and educational leaflets to aid those wishing to grow their own trees. The WDA purchases surplus crops from local growers and makes the frozen fruit available throughout the year to individual consumers and secondary producers.

'Fabulous' – the word used in 1867 to describe the bumper crop quoted above – means fantastical or fictitious; this definition, as well as our modern colloquial usage, may come to mind on a visit to the Lyth Valley during springtime. Nestled among lush green fields glistening from light rain and lacy with white blossoms, the WDA's

> **"** If there is one thing the public goes daffy about it is Damson plums, regular sour Damsons. [...] Ninety per cent, or I might say 98 per cent, of the Damsons here-abouts have been dug up from around the parent trees. [...] Damsons have a peculiar flavor not found in any other plum and they are always sought for by the housewife and the supply rarely equals the demand. [...] While at one time they were a common sight in every chicken yard, the ravages of black knot and a general lack of interest has reduced them to a few families. They should be more widely planted.[35] **"**

At the start of the twentieth century, damsons were 'highly esteemed' in the United States,[36] but as this writer suggests, by the 1920s, they were already falling from favour. Fortunately, a few American nurseries continue to offer trees, mainly the Shropshire variety, in standard and dwarf sizes.

Damson Day beckons, drawing crowds of as many as three thousand visitors over the course of the day.[47] Gin bottles, jam jars, and schoolchildren's artworks display flapping prize ribbons. Stately llamas greet visitors to a tent where their fleece is sold. Artisans construct coracles and willow trellises. Clever dogs soar and swerve through an agility course. Children laugh merrily on rides and take turns cuddling lambs. Dry stone wall techniques are demonstrated. Barns are lined with vendors selling damson everything: savoury damson-studded sourdough loaves, damson bangers, and damson meat pies, as well as traditional damson cakes, chutneys, and cheeses. Locally brewed damson stout is on tap. Orchard tours depart throughout the day on foot. Live music, Crook Morris dancers, and cookery demonstrations fill tents with chatter, laughter, and applause. In its early years, Damson Day was held in Crosthwaite village hall, but the increasingly large crowds required more space. Low Farm became the venue in 2003, and the event has been held there every year since that the weather has permitted. Low Farm owner Anne Wilson also oversees the combined stores of WDA damsons, all grown within a three-mile radius and sold frozen from one of her barns all year round.

Elsewhere in the Lyth Valley, the age-old custom of wassailing has been established to celebrate the damsons. Wassailing, a community ritual performed to promote a good crop of fruit in the coming year, has been ongoing (or reawakened) at numerous cider orchards in Devon, Somerset, Herefordshire, Gloucestershire, Worcestershire, Kent, and Sussex. Wassailing traditions of each area vary, but typically include singing, dancing, drinking, and noise making on Old Twelfth Night (17 January), or at other times around Christmas and New Year.[48] Wassailing done as an agricultural blessing was traditionally a 'magical rite intended to increase yields; [...] even though wassailing took place within a social framework that was Christian, it was demonstrably magical in that it sought to conjure a beneficial outcome through intercession with the trees themselves'.[49] The adaptation of this ritual to Lyth Valley damsons was piloted by Judy Malkin of Kendal, who had the idea of adapting apple wassailing to the local specialty. 'A tradition has to be new once,' she says, explaining that:

> ...as a society we've become disassociated with where our food comes from, and in the past, that's what was most important. People in the past had ceremonies centred mainly around agricultural food, because without that you had nothing. We've lost that, and the idea was to bring that back. To do something that makes you remember where your roots are.[50]

The Lyth Valley wassailing, in its tenth year at the time of writing, has taken place in sun, rain and snow – and anyone is welcome. Though the ceremony varies from year to year, the damson wassailers borrow from apple-wassailing traditions: a Master of Ceremonies addresses the crowd and the tree before pouring some damson beer onto the roots of the tree. Traditionally, the cider poured on tree roots symbolized the 'blood' of the tree, and pouring it on the roots is meant to revive the tree for the coming season. Noise making is thought to ward off evil spirits (such as insects or parasites) and summon the good spirit of the springtime robin.[51] A large, three-handled wassail cup of damson beer is shared, then participants dip bread in what's left of the beer and hang it on the tree, along with festive ribbons. Songs are sung to the tree, and pieces of wassailing cake are distributed. Malkin developed her wassail cake recipe to travel well and feed a crowd: on a large tray she spreads a spiced scone mixture and bakes it until crisp, then she places apple slices and a sweetened damson pulp over the base, and tops it with another layer of scone before baking it further.

After the orchard songs, dances, and rituals are finished, the group retires to a local pub for a meal and more singing, Crook Morris dancing, and revelry. Malkin recalls after the first year of wassailing, the wassailed tree yielded 55 lbs of fruit: 'We thought it was a miracle cure!' The damsons she picks from the blessed tree each year are saved to make the next year's beer and wassail cake, with surplus distributed to ceremony participants. Whether the wassailing ceremony each January influences the chosen tree's yield or not, the adaptation of this time-honoured English ritual shows the sense of community identity damsons inspire and their significance in the natural and cultural landscape. Taffy Thomas, the storyteller of Grasmere, commented on the damson wassailing, 'in this day and age folk find or create the stories and rituals they require to re-state their cultural identity'.[52] Through the vigorous efforts of local enthusiasts, damsons are being recognized as crucial to the identity of the people and landscape of Cumbria.

Since the formation of the WDA, Westmorland damsons have been enjoying a comeback, inspiring chefs and secondary producers across Cumbria with their distinctive flavour. Lyth Valley damsons appear on food and drink menus at inns and restaurants throughout the region, and enrich the offerings of local bakers (such as Ginger Bakers and More? the Artisan Bakery) and jam makers (Claire's Handmade, Friendly Food and Drink, Hawkshead Relish Company, and Wild and Fruitful), some of whom have garnered awards for their damson products. Northern grocery chain Booths offers Lyth Valley damson paste at the cheese counter and seasonal specialities such as Lancashire cheese and damson jelly pastry parcels.

SHROPSHIRE PRUNE DAMSONS

The county of Shropshire has the distinction of being namesake to the most widely available damson cultivar. Damson trees are typical of cottage gardens, orchards, and hedgerows in Shropshire and the surrounding counties of Worcestershire (especially around Tenbury Wells), Herefordshire, and Montgomeryshire, Wales. Spatterings of white blossom may be seen throughout the countryside in these areas, and in late summer damsons appear for sale in markets. The Ludlow area in particular will furnish numerous opportunities for buying Shropshire Prune damsons in season, and local producer/retailer Ludlow Food Centre offers damson products all year round.

Damsons in gardens and hedgerows would have provided a household with ample fruit for the production of jams, pastes, and liqueurs. Until the Second World War, an annual fair was held in

Market Drayton each September for growers to sell their surplus damsons. In her charming survey of traditional foods in and around the town, Meg Pybus recounts:

> The damson in Drayton was prolific, old gnarled damson trees of today have produced their fair quota of fruit for local consumption and particularly for sale at the local Damson Fair held on the seventh to ninth of September (the Nativity of the Virgin Mary on September eighth). [...] Damsons by the buckets and bathfuls were laid out in the market and sold in 90 lb lots. Mark Suthery told me an amusing pre-First World War story of an old lady who came into town to sell a cartful of damsons, was unable to get a good price, so in her fury tipped the whole lot over Cheshire Street! [...] Damson jam in Drayton, especially after a year of 'glut', appears on every larder shelf and charity stall.[53]

A good damson year can be bad news for sellers because prices fall so low. In another account, 'Cheshire Street between The Railway Hotel and the Brewery was ankle-deep with damsons, which the farmers had tipped into the street'[54] after they couldn't be sold.

Shropshire damsons contributed to international relations when King Birenda of Nepal made a state visit to London in November 1980. The king, who had become acquainted with the stiff fruit paste called damson cheese when his wife purchased some at the Royal Show a few years earlier, is said to have requested a menu of roast lamb with damson cheese for a banquet given in his honour. According to May Martin of the Market Drayton Women's Institute, the group 'received the royal command for 2 cwt of damson cheese to be made in the remarkably short time of two days. Organised by Judy Boffey, freezers were raided, and the band of WI ladies had made, packed into jars and delivered, this vast quantity to the Agriculture House in London, from where it was transported to the Guildhall, just in time for the banquet, only forty-eight hours later'.[55]

From 1987 through the mid-1990s, the damson fair was

remembered with an annual Damson Feast at Goldstone Hall, a country house hotel outside Market Drayton. Menus from these feasts show such appetizing offerings as wild boar sausage and damson pickle, mushrooms stuffed with chicken mousseline in a damson wine sauce, English lamb with a damson-pineapple-mint glaze, and damson beignets on a white peach coulis.[56] Hotel proprietor John Cushing says, 'things like damson cheese are very important […] and you need chefs who are interested in doing that sort of thing. To an extent, it's a lost skill'. Though the Damson Feast is no longer held at the hotel, Cushing continues to grow

DAMSONS IN LITERATURE

Jonathon Green, in his *Green's Dictionary of Slang*, defines 'damson-pie' as 'obscene language,' possibly a pun on the exclamation 'damn!' An example can be found in Glaswegian novelist William Black's *The Strange Adventures of a House-boat* (1888): '…even if you were to hear some of the Birmingham lads giving each other a dose of "damson-pie" – that is the polite name they have for it – you wouldn't understand a single sentence'. A 1975 collection of poems by English poet Bernard Gutteridge bears the title *Old Damson-Face*, conjuring images of an unhealthy complexion or sour expression.

Predictably, the damson features in folklore of the Lyth Valley. 'The Jamming Pan,' a story told by Richard Harrison of Low Fell, Crosthwaite in 1938, unfolds during damson time.[37] The occupants of a remote farm must travel five or six miles to borrow a brass pan for jamming from a neighbor. The farmer grudgingly fetches the pan himself, but vows that he will not be the one to return it. After the jam is made, he proposes that the first in the family to speak must return the pan. The family falls silent. When a tramp comes upon the house, he helps himself to food and cash, surprised that no one speaks a word of protest. Making bold, he kisses the farmer's wife and daughter, still without anyone voicing an objection. The farmer won't speak up to defend the honour of his wife or daughter, but when the visitor approaches the farmer himself for a kiss, the silence is broken damsons on the grounds, and to include damson cheese, chutney, and crumble on his menus.

A ubiquitous feature in Salopian hedgerows and gardens, damsons unsurprisingly also feature in the material culture of the area. In the eighteenth century, the soft-paste porcelain manufacturer Caughley of Broseley, Shropshire, produced a design (1777-1784) in underglaze blue called 'Apples and Damsons,' featuring these two local fruits.[57] Damsons are depicted on the embroidered valances and counterpane designed for the Corbet Bed (1593), built for Sir Andrew Corbet of Moreton Corbet Castle, near Shawbury. Between 1997 and 2010,

as the farmer exclaims, 'Nay, damn it. I'll tek t'pan back!' Storyteller Taffy Thomas of Grasmere tells the tale of 'The Magic Orchard', in which a damson tree protects a young girl after apple and pear trees refuse to hide her from a witch.

In Rick Schreiter's 1967 children's book, *The Delicious Plums of King Oscar the Bad*, a young boy who loves damson jelly is distraught when the tyrannical monarch, King Oscar, cuts off his village's supply of damsons from the private royal tree. The boy sets out in a hot air balloon to entreat the king to reconsider. Upon discovering the boy attempting to pluck a damson from the tree, King Oscar laments that he is forced to eat damsons daily by the domineering queen, and yearns for a preserve of any other fruit. As it turns out, the young boy has in his satchel a jar of his mother's lemon marmalade, the tedious food *he's* been forced to eat. King Oscar, his mood elevated by the relief of eating lemon marmalade, permits the boy to fill his satchel with damsons. The frontispiece of the book serves as a prologue, depicting the revelry that predates the king's revocation of the damson harvest: villagers of all ages clutch jam-smeared toasts, carve up slices of damson pie, tend to a massive jelly bag of pink liquid, and brandish spoonfuls of damson pudding amid baskets, crates, and firkins brimming with plump blue damsons. The theme of bounty followed by scarcity is familiar to anyone who grows or loves damsons.

a team of intrepid volunteer embroiderers, under the guidance of plant heritage expert Margaret Owen and descendant Leila Corbet, created new curtains, valances, and counterpane for the bed, based on Owen's meticulously researched patterns. Inspired by textile designs of the time in the Victoria & Albert Museum collections, the bed valances depict sixteenth-century orchards containing damson and bullace trees, and the counterpane features a branch bearing purply-blue damson plums, among other botanical motifs. The bed, on loan from the V&A, and hung with its new tapestries, is displayed at Shrewsbury Museum and Art Gallery.[58]

Shropshire is home to the national damson collection, which is located in Coalbrookdale Arboretum, close to the Darby Houses at the Coalbrookdale Museum of Iron in Telford. Planted in 1993 with specimens donated by the National Council for the Conservation of Plants and Gardens,[59] the initial scheme included six damson varieties, seven bullace varieties, and two mirabelles. Collection curator Gillian Crumpton explains: 'Coalbrookdale has always had damsons, you'll see them in hedgerows and everywhere, they've got a strong local provenance; they're synonymous with this area.'[60] Different groups have been responsible for the orchard's care through the years, a number of trees have been replaced, and work was recently needed to enhance light and airflow to the existing trees. Plans are underway to expand the collection (adding varieties not yet represented) and improve access for visitors, who are welcome to enjoy the fruit when it ripens each year.

In 2010, the Slow Food convivium based in Ludlow successfully saw the Shropshire Prune damson accepted to the 'Ark of Taste,' a designation that brings attention to traditional, seasonal foods at risk of being forgotten. Through publicity, education, and a web presence, the group seeks to promote the brand identity and use of this heritage fruit. The group sponsors a series of 'taste workshops' during Ludlow Food Festival to educate chefs and others who are interested in working with damsons. Chairperson Sue Chantler says they all have great affection for the Shropshire prune, which remains a constant fixture on meeting agendas and special event dinner menus.

Hedgerow damsons and bullaces are 'wild, seasonal, and ephemeral,' Chantler explains, and people have to 'use it or lose it'.[61]

*

Over time, many damson orchards have been grubbed out and hedgerows removed to make way for large farm machinery or land development. In response, community groups, heritage workers, and individuals are stepping up to restore and replace orchards, educate the public, and advocate for forgotten, local foods. Community organizations can follow the lead of Shropshire Hills Discovery Centre in Craven Arms, where traditional hedgerows including damsons, sloes, raspberries, and currants have been planted around their meadows. The Centre's 'Discovery Club' participants (children aged between three and seven) are guided in learning about and enjoying the fruit.[62]

At historic sites where damsons still grow, a pick-your-own scheme can provide additional income. At Brockhampton Estate, a National Trust property in Herefordshire, close to three hundred Merryweather and Shropshire Prune damson trees, plus those in the hedgerows, are maintained in traditional ways. The oldest trees are between fifty and sixty years old, and are replaced as they die off. The orchards are managed to promote biodiversity, with wide spacing of trees, fruit harvesting by hand, and no use of fertilizers or pesticides. During a four-week window, locals and visitors from nearby cities come to buy damsons. Ranger Nick Hinchliffe says that some people who come to pick damsons may remember them from when they were younger, but don't have a garden now, or can't manage their own trees. About 80% of the damsons sold are pick-your-own.

Grassroots movements have been launched by individuals with an interest in heritage and the natural environment. In Bedfordshire, Steve Halton of Central Bedfordshire Council began working on a 'Damsons in Distress' project in 2008 (the name was later changed to 'Prunes in Peril'). Damsons occur in a chalky, damp, low-lying area across the county boundaries of Bedfordshire and Buckinghamshire, bounded by the villages of Totternhoe, Pitstone and Cheddington. The fruit grew here robustly between 1910 and 1940, but, as elsewhere, production dwindled during the 1950s. These damsons are known locally by the name 'Aylesbury Prune' (despite the plum literature identifying Aylesbury Prune as a *domestica* variety).[63] Halton's plans include surveying existing orchards and planting new ones, collecting oral histories, and promoting the fruit through school activities, public events, and educational materials.[64] This project, like so many of its kind, requires time and resources to persist, so progress has been slow.

Orchards are being created, regenerated, and preserved through the efforts of individuals and groups who find value in food that is locally grown, seasonal, and traditional. Such efforts restore the rich biodiversity of orchard habitats, maintain the characteristic look of the landscape, and ensure damsons will be plentiful and accessible for years to come.

ADVICE FOR GROWING, BUYING AND STORING DAMSONS

Growing Damsons

For those who don't have the good fortune to live in a damson-growing region, a single tree in the garden can provide ample fruit for the household. Damsons are long-lived, so planting one is a gift to the next generation. Nick Dunn,[1] proprietor of Frank P. Matthews nursery in the West Midlands, sells six different varieties of damson and bullace. Dunn estimates that 90% of damson trees he sells go into gardens, though occasionally a commercial grower will plant a damson orchard. Most damson trees sold today will have been vegetatively propagated; a cutting is taken from the desired damson variety and grafted onto a reliable rootstock. Rootstocks are selected for their compatibility with the damson, their tolerance for diverse soil types, and their disinclination to produce suckers. Damsons are best planted in the spring, and reset, if needed, in the late fall or early winter.

Replanting of suckers that shoot up from the base of older trees is a method of propagation practiced in Cumbria, and is advisable only if the parent tree was not grafted, since the suckers emerge from the rootstock. Trees from suckers will mature and fruit sooner than those grown from seed (in about eight years) and the fruit will be genetically identical to the fruit of the tree from which the sucker was taken. Suckered damsons are ideal for planting in hedgerows, spaced eight to ten metres apart, mixed in with sloe, blackberry, elderberry and other edibles. Including damsons in new hedgerow plantings is a wonderful way to add utility and beauty: a row of damson saplings will develop into a dense windbreak, providing blossoms in the spring and fruits in the fall. Scottish landscape planner and garden writer John Claudius Loudon, who advised that attention be paid to the aesthetics of labourers' cottages and gardens 'for the sake of the inhabitants' well-being and productivity', recommends enclosing the pig-sty with 'a holly, thorn, sloe-thorn, or damson-plum hedge, according to circumstances'.[2]

Damsons are tremendously tolerant, but they have their preferences if they are to live a vigorous and fruitful life. Plums planted on a southern slope will produce a better yield, but those on northern slopes are less likely to blossom too early and suffer frost damage. East-facing slopes are preferred to west.[3] The trees require moisture-retentive soil that is not waterlogged. Soils composed primarily of peat and clay are to be avoided. Soil amendments for damsons might include a top dressing of ashes or coal dust, to discourage weed growth (the tar in these substances will scorch the weeds). 'A quart can of salt cast under each tree before the hoe begins, every year or two' discourages insects that require an underground period in their life cycle.[4] Liberal use of bone meal will benefit the tree, because 'the many seeds which the tree must perfect demands it'.[5] H.V. Taylor recommends 'annual dressings of dung or like substances to maintain fertility, and more particularly to conserve water supplies. Substantial dressings of nitrogenous fertilisers should also be given and occasionally a dressing of lime'.[6] Seek advice for growing damsons in your geographic area and climate. You may benefit from having your soil analysed. I was shocked to learn how acidic and inhospitable the soil in my orchard was, and have remedied this with applications of lime.

Damsons are self-fertile, so only one tree is required to produce fruit. They tend to grow all over the place, and older trees develop charismatic, gnarled shapes. If planted in groups, allow at least eight metres between trees to permit free airflow and full light. Damsons do not do well in forest settings or any place that is shaded or stagnant. I've witnessed a rather sad damson growing on espalier wires: the owner had started with two and one had already died. When he consulted the Royal Horticultural Society postmortem, they explained that plum trees don't like being forced to grow in a certain way. Being trained around the wire puts strain on the bark, weakening it; those weakened spots can open up and create a gap vulnerable to fungus.

Damsons are relatively resistant to canker, pests, and disease (as are bullaces and sloes), but they are not invulnerable to attack. Fungal infections can devastate a tree or its harvest. Black knot, identified by bubbly black galls encrusting limbs and ultimately killing them, is caused by the fungus *Apiosporina morbosa*. Silver Leaf fungus, caused by *Chondrostereum purpureum*, appears as a rubbery bracket-shaped growth on the tree and causes leaves of affected areas to take on a silver colour. 'Bent Banana' or 'Pocket plum' disease is caused by the fungus *Taphrina pruni*. Damp, warm weather in early spring creates conditions conducive to the spread of this fungus. In a series of increasingly disturbing transformations, the damsons become spotted, then overly large, then elongated, withered, yellowed and bent, before turning grey and dropping, having never developed a stone.[7] Aphids will feed on damson foliage, creating a curled leaf appearance; the 'Damson-hop aphid' (*Phorodon humuli*) is of particular concern. In North America, the curculio weevil lays eggs in developing fruit, leaving a telltale crescent-shaped scar. Permitting hogs or chickens to browse under the damson trees makes the ground inhospitable for this pest, as it requires undisturbed soil to complete its reproductive cycle.[8]

Ohio plum farmer Eliphas Cope, author of *A Practical Treatise on Plum Growing* (1888), beseeches the plum grower to 'care for them [the trees] the same as a horse or cow',[9] and while such close care might be beneficial, damsons have a long history of making it on their own, growing 'half-wild, thriving with little or no care'.[10]

When it comes time to harvest, the tedious work begins. 'Alas, good master, my wife desired some damsons / And made me climb, with danger of my life', says Simpcox to Gloucester in Shakespeare's *Henry VI, Part 2*. Why might one be in danger of one's life picking damsons? The damson's twiggy, sometimes spiny branches can scratch, and brittle limbs of older trees are notorious for splitting. A heavy snow or a heavy load of fruit can bring down a branch. When a tree can snap under the weight of its own crop, it is surely unsuitable for supporting a human climber. And yet, Meg Pybus of Shropshire recalls a valiant elderly acquaintance who would climb the old gnarled damson tree in her garden until she'd picked the very last plum. Spreading a cloth under the tree and shaking the fruit loose has been suggested, but fruit may be bruised in the process.[11] A ladder can be used to reach the centre of the tree; for the spreading outer branches, one may stand on a tractor or quad bike, repositioning as needed. Damson picking is a plodding process, regardless of the method employed.

Depending on the variety and where in the world they are growing, damsons may come ripe as early as mid-August; others will be harvested well into October. For making jam, it is best to use plums a day or two ahead of full ripeness for a higher pectin content.[12] Almost ripe damsons will require a tug to release from the tree. A fully ripe plum will detach with little effort, and by the final days of the harvest, the slightest touch will cause them to drop. A ripe plum will have the best flavour and sweetness (to the extent that damsons get sweet), but ripe fruit is also more prone to bruising and insect damage, and must be used without delay.[13]

Buying Damsons

If all this talk of brittle branches and bent bananas does not inspire, damsons may be purchased already grown, at the right place, at the right time. Damsons are seasonable in the UK in September and October. They should be easily found fresh in season in Cumbria, Shropshire, Cheshire, Worcestershire, and Herefordshire, at roadside stands or in farm markets. The Westmorland Damson Association sells frozen damsons all year round. Purchase firm, unblemished fruits with a translucent bloom gracing the blue-black skins. Frozen damsons will have a shinier, more purplish appearance. For individuals who love the fruit, its potential scarcity in any given year, or abundance in another, makes harvesting (or buying) damsons a special occasion.

Storing Damsons

Before storing damsons, remove stems and leaves, and wash and dry the fruit thoroughly. Remove any bruised or compromised fruit. For short-term storage, ripe damsons may be stored in the refrigerator (I've had success keeping them this way for over a month). Refrigerate damsons in plastic bags to prevent them drying out and shrivelling, but leave the bags open to permit some airflow.

For long-term storage, damsons may be frozen whole in airtight containers. For most uses, frozen do just as well as fresh if they are frozen promptly and used immediately after thawing. Thawed damsons will be softer and juicier than fresh, and will give up their stones more easily. For less work later on, cook and sieve the damsons to make a purée before freezing. Tablespoon-size portions of purée may be frozen in ice cube trays then popped out into freezer bags. A few 500-gram portions can go into freezer bags too, with all air pushed out before sealing. These can be flattened and stacked in the freezer. Damson purée may be added to condiments, apple sauces, and a variety of puddings. The sweetened version is easily thawed to enliven ice cream, cheesecake, Eton Mess, trifle, or cake.

Unsweetened Damson Purée to Freeze

Simmer clean, ripe damsons with a little water (to prevent sticking before they release their juice) for 10-20 minutes. Rub through a sieve to remove stones and skins. If pulp is runnier than desired, return to a clean pan over medium-low heat, stirring frequently until the desired consistency is reached.

Sweetened Damson Purée to Freeze

As per preceding recipe, but when the desired consistency is reached stir in a quarter to a third their initial weight in granulated or caster sugar over low heat until dissolved.

Dried Damsons

There is historical evidence to suggest that plums from Damascus were dried in the sun (as other plums were) in ancient times, though whether they were damsons is not certain. In experiments with a home food dryer, I found that raw halved damsons were mostly dry after twelve hours, whereas whole fruits took twenty-four hours or longer. The skins became quite tough. Dried damsons would perhaps be agreeable chopped fine in a fruit cake, but there are easier, better ways to preserve damsons.

DAMSON RECIPES

INTRODUCTION

In my conversations with damson growers and enthusiasts, jams and gins are predictably mentioned as favourite things to make with damsons. Multiple recipes for each are included here. But to only make jams and gins would not 'plumb' the full potential of the damson's utility. From cinnamony streusel-topped damson traybake, to rich damson ice cream, to gingery damson tomato spread, this diverse sampling of new and old recipes showcases the damson's versatility. Some have been collected from people who know and love damsons, some are historical, resurrected from time-worn cookery books, and some are original. Experiment, and you will find that damsons deliciously swap with tart fruits or berries in familiar dishes and condiments. The recipes collected herein celebrate damson dishes from English kitchens past, and embrace damsons as a key ingredient in our kitchens today.

A NOTE ABOUT MEASUREMENTS

Historic recipes can seem threadbare to those of us accustomed to the precise methods, temperatures, and timings of today's recipes. Where needed, I have annotated historic recipes with suggested times, temperatures, and quantities. Historic recipes are reprinted in their original form in most cases, so measurement systems used will vary. For teaspoons and tablespoons, I have not distinguished between US and UK spoons, despite a slight difference in their volumes. In years of cooking from British books using American measuring spoons, I have never found this to be a difference that makes a difference.

A Note About Sugar

Damsons are famous for their tartness, but the astringency of a particular crop depends on variety, ripeness, weather, and other variables. Damsons picked after a frost will be milder, and refrigeration/freezing can slightly dull their brightness. Bullaces typically require more sugar than damsons to be palatable. You will need to taste and adjust sugar accordingly. An exception is for jams and jellies being prepared for long-term storage. Sugar is an important factor in inhibiting bacterial growth; the sugar-to-fruit ratio of these recipes should not be radically altered.

A Note about Food Safety

Food science is a fascinating field with high stakes findings. Many of the historical recipes included in this collection were written before Nicolas Appert's invention of heat-processing for foods in the nineteenth century. 'Open-kettle canning,' or 'bottling' methods from the past prescribe filling jars with hot jam or fruit and relying on the product's heat to seal them. Jams potted in this way often develop surface mould, because microbes already on the food and jar, or in the air, persist, and the seal may not be strong enough to keep new organisms out. *Clostridium botulinum* is a bacterium that causes botulism, and while it does not flourish in acidic or sugary environments, mould growth on the surface of a food can gradually raise the food's pH, allowing toxins to develop. Consumers have long assumed that scraping away visible mould will render a product safe to consume, but if the mould has altered the acidity of the food in the anaerobic environment of a closed jar, botulinum toxins may be present. Heat-processing filled jars will kill existing microbes and seal the jars securely to keep new ones out.[1]

Many of the recipes here are scaled down to be made with a kilogram or less of fruit – a jar to give and one to keep – used over the course of a few weeks and stored in the refrigerator. When 'putting up' large quantities for long-term storage, heat-process the filled jars. For jam, this typically means ladling hot jam into jars designed specifically for heat-processing, allowing 1 cm headspace between the food and the rim of the jar, wiping the rim clean, and affixing a metal two-part lid before processing in a boiling water bath. For jam, ten to fifteen minutes in a boiling water bath will inhibit microbial growth; for apple sauces and lower acid/lower sugar products, fifteen to twenty minutes is typically recommended. Check the seals on the jars after twenty-four hours. Jars that failed to seal may be reprocessed (wipe the rim and try again with a fresh lid) or stored in the refrigerator for immediate use. Ongoing research may yield new advice for home canners; consult an up-to-date, credible source before processing your jars.

Open-kettle, bottling, and wax disc methods are not recommended by the National Center for Home Food Preservation (US), or by any other reputable agency concerned with food safety. Large-batch home canning is more prevalent in the United States than in the United Kingdom, which is why much of our knowledge about food safety in home canning comes from US sources. For a well-researched account of why heat-processing is crucial, with explanations written especially for skeptical UK cooks, see www.healthycanning.com. I urge you to benefit from twentieth- and twenty-first-century food research and ensure your home-made foods are safe for yourselves and your loved ones.

Jams, Jellies, and Preserves

Damson jams, jellies, and preserves invigorate the breakfast or tea table, and provide ready fillings for Victoria sandwich, linzertortes, kolaches, tartlets, and so much more. H.V. Taylor dismisses *domestica* plums as lacking 'character' in jam, but the exceptional damson 'has a character sufficiently distinctive' for this use.[2] May Byron, compiler of the 1915 cookery book *Pot-Luck*, expresses a strong prejudice for home-made jam:

> The great pre-eminence of the home jam over the factory article, is that, in the words of Sam Weller, one 'knows the lady wot made it'. One also is assured that she did not put in carrots, seeds, glucose, or any alien matter in the way of coloratives, preservatives, or sweeteners unknown to the 'home-farm'. Of home-made jam one may partake freely with pleasant and beneficial results; shop jam frequently leaves an acid taste in the mouth and a most undesirable effect upon the whole of the mucous membrane. Jams and preserves, moreover, can be so easily achieved, and in most cases so cheaply, that one is hardly justified in denying one's family these inexpensive and invaluable commodities.[3]

Sugar makes astringent damsons more palatable, but many commercial damson jams contain too much, and, in so doing, suppress the damson's vivacity. Tartness is desirable in jams being dolloped on cream-mounded scones and butter-slathered crumpets; a balance of contrasting flavours cannot be achieved with a too-sugary jam. Damsons contain ample pectin to set without adding gelling agents. Really, all one needs is fruit and sugar.

Supplies and tips for jams, jellies, and fruit butters

An official jamming pan is not required; any heavy-bottomed pan with adequate volume for the amount of fruit will do. I find that enamelled cast iron works well for even heating. Ensure before starting that you have enough sound, heatproof jars and lids. Some cooks routinely repurpose old jars with screw-on lids from the grocery store, but for the safest preservation, proper canning jars and lids with new, fresh seals or gaskets are recommended. A ladle or Pyrex jug is useful for filling jars; special spouted jam ladles are a nice treat if you find yourself making jam regularly. A jar funnel is an inexpensive tool that will make the jar-filling process tidier. If making jelly, a jelly bag or fine strainer is required to drain the juice from the pulp. Damson skins tend to stick to the pan (and can potentially catch), so I use a spade-shaped silicone spatula with a thin, flexible edge to constantly squeegee the bottom of the pan, rather than simply stirring. This method allows me to be aware when a channel can be drawn through the mixture (a sign of doneness), and when making smaller batches I can be assured that nothing is sticking as I glimpse the white enamel pan bottom with each pass.

First-time jam-makers may benefit from the company of an experienced friend who can help manage boiling fruit, hot glass, and setting point anxiety. I admit to being an anxious jam-maker; I tend to hover over my jamming pan, having overcooked more than a few batches waiting for the right temperature to register on an untrustworthy thermometer, or from inattention. Mrs Beeton advises caution: 'Jams require the same care and attention in the boiling as marmalade; the slightest degree of burning communicates a disagreeable empyreumatic taste, and if they are not boiled sufficiently, they will not keep.' Even if it doesn't catch, the flavour of an over-boiled jam will be 'off', and the set may be disagreeably firm.

Jams and jellies will usually gel when they reach a temperature of 105 C / 220 F, but this standard may vary depending on the particular mix of fruit, sugar, and other ingredients. Keep watch on the thermometer, but, to be safe, employ visual techniques for assessing doneness as well. My preferred visual technique for plums is to drag a silicone spatula or spoon across the bottom of the pan and look for a channel to appear, then quickly vanish. You may also observe the formation of droplets off a raised spoon (looking for a single, wide-based drop rather than multiple dribbly thin drips). While your pan is off the heat, you can dollop some jam on a cold plate and pop it in the freezer for a minute to see how it will behave when cool; if the cooled dollop wrinkles when prodded, it's ready. My grandmother's trick was to place a small mound of jam on a plate and observe whether a thin ring of transparent juice formed around its perimeter. If the mound shows clean, defined edges, the jam is done. These experiments should be conducted with the pan off the heat source, to avoid overcooking during that crucial moment when you are deciding whether it's perfectly set. It's easy to return the jam to the boil after a quick test. One can always boil jam more if testing reveals it isn't done, but never less once it's been overcooked.

The fashion of late for small-batch canning of preserves and jams is a sign of our times. We may recall our grandmothers processing bushel upon bushel of seasonal fruit and lining their larders with uniform jars of preserved veg and fruit, but contemporary life has made such undertakings the stuff of legends. For those of us with smaller families and less time for food preparation, traditions like jam-making can be carried on if we scale down. A small batch can be refrigerated and enjoyed at once, with a jar to spare for a friend. I've included some original historical recipes in their generous proportions, but there are also a number of recipes with smaller yields. When halving or doubling any recipe, be aware that cooking times will fluctuate with the volume of the batch.

Damson jams and jellies of fine quality may be procured from farm shops, but I join the chorus of wise women who have written before me that there is no comparison between an industrial supermarket product and a home-made jam. The flavours of a home-made jam are brighter, and the texture 'fruitier' and less uniform. There's an intangible satisfaction in creating something lasting from something ephemeral, to being able to 'capture the magic of seasonal fruit and hold it in suspension for months (or even years) to come'.[4]

In a world in which our 'to do lists' are rarely finished we may take pride in toiling a few hours to produce tidy, colourful jars to savour and to give. Once your jam is potted, you may wish to follow novelist and kitchen essayist Laurie Colwin's suggestion for home canning, and arrange your jars 'in a nice little row to remind yourself what a wonderful person you are'.[5]

DAMSON BUTTERS

In 1941, Ruth E. Arthur wrote to the 'Homemaker' column in the Toronto *Globe and Mail* newspaper[6] enquiring about an English recipe her mother had made called Damson cheese: 'The jam was quite firm,' Ms Arthur writes, 'it was cooked for a long time, I remember.' The Homemaker columnist responded with several recipes for plum 'butter', a North American term for a thick fruit spread. On the spectrum of fruit pastes, butter is considerably softer than cheese, which holds its shape and can be sliced. Fruit butters in North America are commonly made from the pulp of apples or pumpkins, but this chapter begins, as the notion to write this book did, with my family recipe for the damson preserves we called 'Plum Butter'.

DAMSON 'PLUM BUTTER'

This recipe for a thick, pulpy damson spread was made by my grandfather's grandmother, Rose, by Rose's daughter-in-law, Jennie, and by Jennie's daughter-in-law, Marcella (my grandmother). I remember sitting at the kitchen table every September, watching my grandmother patiently stir the huge pot of damsons for hours. Then there was a flurry of jar-filling as steam from the water-bath canner filled the kitchen. Further waiting was required as the jam cooled, sounding a crisp chorus of pops, as metal lids sealed successfully. Late summer crickets and cicadas sang outside and dizzy moths fluttered against the kitchen windowpane as a cooled jar was at last opened that evening. I've included the original recipe as well as an updated version that saves time by pre-chopping the damsons with a food processor.

Large Batch (original recipe, cooks for several hours, yields 6 pints)
3 kg / 6 lb damsons (stones removed before weighing)
1 litre / 1 ¾ pints water
1 kg / 2 lb sugar

Combine all ingredients in a large, heavy-bottomed pot over medium heat. As damsons begin to turn burgundy, stir with increasing frequency to prevent the bottom from catching. As the mixture thickens, constant stirring is required. Test for doneness as indicated below.

Small Batch (more manageable, cooks in 30 minutes, yields ¾ pint)
500 g / 1 lb damsons (stones removed before weighing)
125 ml / 4 fl oz / ½ cup water
125 g / 4 oz granulated sugar

Place all ingredients in the bowl of a food processor and pulse until the damson skins become small flecks (do this several times in succession if making a larger batch). Transfer to a large, heavy-bottomed pan and simmer until the mixture is thick and dark, taking care to stir frequently to prevent catching. (Even the small batch will start to stick after only a few minutes.) Reduce heat if the mixture begins to spatter. To test doneness, use the channel method described in the chapter introduction, or spoon a small mound onto a plate. If a thin perimeter of juice forms at the base of the mound, further cooking is required. Fill jars and heat-process if desired.

GLOBE AND MAIL DAMSON JELLY AND BUTTER (2 IN 1)

The next pair of recipes comes from Toronto's *Globe and Mail* newspaper (1941), with the handy suggestion of turning leftover pulp from jelly-making into fruit butter, with just a bit of additional work. Nothing goes to waste! This jelly is pure damson, dazzlingly clear. The butter is made from sieved pulp, so it is smoother in texture than the recipe above.

Wash and prick Damsons, put in preserving kettle with just enough water to keep fruit from burning. Cook slowly until fruit is soft, then rub it through a coarse sieve. Then drain through a jelly bag. Measure juice, bring to boiling point, boil for five minutes, then add three-quarters as much heated sugar as you had juice, stir, and again bring to the boiling point. Boil for three minutes, skim, and pour into sterilized jelly glasses.

After covering/canning these jelly jars, return to that bag of pulp. Rub the pulp through a sieve, or remove stones by hand. Measure the amount of pulp produced, then:

Add the juice of one lemon for each 2 cups, add spices to taste, and 2 cups sugar for each 3 cups of pulp. Simmer slowly […]. Care should be taken that the product does not scorch.

HONEYED DAMSON BUTTER

Commonly found in Cumbrian orchard walls,[7] bee boles (shelters for bees) support a symbiotic partnership between fruit blossoms and the pollinators that facilitate fruiting. Because jams made with honey don't stay fresh as long as those made with sugar, this recipe makes a small batch (approximately 350 ml) for a decadent long weekend of breakfasts. This is one of the less-sweet jams in the book, permitting the bold tartness of the damsons to shine. Wonderful on thick, strained yoghurt or warm scones. The honey flavour will become more evident once the butter has cooled.

500 g / 1 lb damsons, stones removed, fruit chopped small (pulse in the food processor if you have one)
150 g / 5 oz honey
dash of cinnamon

Combine the ingredients and allow to rest for at least an hour, preferably overnight. Over medium heat, boil the mixture until it thickens and the colour deepens (about 15 minutes). Stir constantly to ensure no bits of skin catch on the bottom of the pan as the liquid evaporates.

Damson Conserve for Ladies

In *Delightes for Ladies* (1609 edition), Sir Hugh Plat prescribes boiling damsons in either wine or rose water before sieving them, cooking the pulp, and sweetening it. The following adaptation makes a smaller batch than the original recipe, with the same ratio of wine to damsons plus a splash of rose water at the end. This floral-perfumed damson butter does well spread between cake layers, or served at an afternoon tea.

1 kg / 2 lb damsons
250 ml / 8 fl oz / 1 cup red wine
sugar equal to the pulp produced
1-2 teaspoons rose water

Boil the damsons in the wine until they are very soft, and the stones have come free from the pulp. Transfer to a fine sieve and rub the flesh and skins through until only stones remain. Weigh the pulp. In a clean pan, combine the pulp with an equal weight of granulated sugar over medium heat. Stir constantly. When sugar has dissolved, add rose water. Bring to a simmer and after five minutes, begin testing, cooking until the desired set has been achieved.

Damson Jams

Eliza Acton's 'Damson Jam (Very Good)'

Acton's jam recipe is written for 6 lbs of damsons and 3 lbs of sugar. Remove stones prior to cooking. If using thawed damsons, the stones will release more easily.

The fruit for this jam should be freshly gathered and quite ripe. Split, stone, weigh, and boil it quickly for forty minutes; then stir in half its weight of good sugar roughly powdered, and when it is dissolved, give the preserve fifteen minutes additional boiling, keeping it stirred, and thoroughly skimmed. A more refined preserve is made by pressing the fruit through a sieve after it is boiled tender; but the jam is excellent without.

Mrs Beeton's Damson Jam

Mrs Beeton's jam recipe is slightly sweeter:

Have the fruit gathered in dry weather; pick it over, and reject any that is at all blemished. Stone the damsons, weigh them, and to every lb allow ¾ lb of loaf sugar. Put the fruit and sugar into a preserving-pan; keep stirring them gently until the sugar is dissolved, and carefully remove the scum as it rises. Boil the jam for about an hour, reckoning from the time it commences to simmer all over alike: it must be well stirred all the time, or it will be liable to burn and stick to the pan, which will cause the jam to have a very disagreeable flavour. When the jam looks firm, and the juice appears to set, it is done. Then take it off the fire, put into pots, cover it down, when quite cold [...] store it away in a dry place.

Plum and Damson Jam with Star Anise

The notion of blending tart damsons with sweeter, more mellow plums comes from a copy of *The Ideal Cookery Book* (c. 1910-19) held by the Wellcome Library in London. I've updated the recipe by reducing the sugar and adding the complementary flavour of star anise. This recipe yields approximately 350 ml of jam, a perfect amount for enjoying over a week or two without heat-processing for long-term use. Remember how many star anise you use so you can retrieve them before potting.

250 g / 8 oz each plums and damsons, weighed after the stones have been removed
225 g / 7 ½ oz granulated sugar
3 whole star anise

Chop the fruit up small, making the plum pieces and damson pieces of uniform size. Combine with sugar and star anise. Let rest several hours, or, ideally, overnight. In a heavy-bottomed pan, heat to a bubbling simmer and cook until set, about 15 minutes. When done, a spatula dragged along the bottom of the pan will leave a channel that does not immediately fill back in.

DAMSON JELLIES

DAMSON JELLY WITH APPLES, GOOSEBERRIES, AND QUINCES

This 1830 damson jelly from Richard Dolby prescribes a flexible assortment of fruits to complement the damsons and soften their intensity. Crab-apples or cranberries would work just as well as the suggested mix of green apples, green gooseberries, and quince cores. Depending on the juiciness of the fruits used, you may need to add a little water to prevent them sticking as they soften. Of all my damson jams and jellies, this is my mother's favourite.

> To eight pounds of damsons, put eight pounds of fine sugar, and half a pint of water; boil them for half an hour over a gentle fire, till the skins break; then take them off, and put them by for an hour; set them on the fire again, for half an hour more; set them by again for the same time; do so the third time; while they stand off the fire, put a weight upon

them to keep them under the syrup. The last time, you must boil them till you perceive they are of a very high colour in the part where the skin is broken; then take them off, set them by to cool, and when they are cold, drain off the syrup, and make the jelly in the following manner: Boil a good quantity of green apples, green gooseberries, and quince cores, to a mash; then strain them through a hair sieve. Take an equal quantity of this jelly and the former syrup, and boil them over a gentle fire together till they jelly; skim it well, and while it is hot, put it into glasses or pots.

Damson Raspberry Jelly

This jelly possesses a gorgeous ruby-magenta colour. The raspberry flavour will be prominent, with a background of damson. If desired, the remaining pulp in the jelly bag may be made into a silky tart 'butter' following the *Globe and Mail* recipe above. The raspberry seeds will be barely noticeable.

750 g / 1 ½ lb damsons
300 g / 10 oz frozen red raspberries
30 ml / 1 fl oz / ⅛ cup lemon juice
granulated sugar to equal the weight of the strained juice

Over medium heat, cook the damsons with lemon juice until soft. Add raspberries and cook until they have broken down. Strain through a jelly bag. Weigh juice, and bring to the boil. Boil for 5 minutes, then add an equal weight of granulated sugar and bring to the boil again. Boil for 3-5 minutes, or until a temperature of 105 C / 220 F is reached. Skim off any foam and transfer to jars for heat-processing or immediate use.

Damson Gin Jelly with Aromatics

This tangy damson jelly incorporates gin, ginger, and juniper. Cloudy like a damson butter, it possesses the versatility to accompany meats or fill a cake, and makes a bright addition to the brunch table.

> *1 kg / 2 lb damsons*
> *50 ml / 1 ¾ fl oz / ¼ cup water*
> *3 kaffir lime leaves*
> *30 g / 1 oz ginger root, cut into thin slices*
> *1 small cinnamon stick*
> *5 whole juniper berries, crushed*
> *350 g / 12 oz granulated sugar*
> *25 ml / 1 fl oz / ⅛ cup lime juice*
> *25 ml / 1 fl oz / ⅛ cup gin*

Bring damsons, water, ginger root, lime leaves and spices to the boil. Reduce heat and simmer for 30 minutes, stirring occasionally. Remove leaves and cinnamon stick. Rub through a fine sieve to remove remaining stones, skins, and spices. In a clean pan, combine the pulp and lime juice. Cook for a further 50-60 minutes at a gentle heat until the mixture is thick. Add sugar and cook a further 5 minutes. Remove from heat and test the set. If satisfactory, stir in gin, and transfer to a jar or serving dish.

Preserves of Whole Damsons

Instructions for preserving or bottling whole damsons for future use occur frequently in cookery books from the seventeenth through nineteenth centuries, before freezing became the easiest option. Mrs Beeton and her contemporaries poured boiling water over damsons in dry stone jars, placed a paper circle on the surface of the liquid, and sealed the paper with melted mutton suet. 'When used,' Beeton instructs, 'the suet should be removed, the water poured off, and the jelly at the bottom of the jar used and mixed with the fruit.' A few decades earlier, Mrs Dalgairns prepared 'Damsons for Winter Use' in a more appealing manner: 'Gather the damsons when just ripe, and perfectly sound; fill a two-gallon brandy keg, and pour over two pounds of treacle; close the keg firmly, and turn it every day.'

Sweetened preserves made with whole fruits lend themselves to a range of uses. Drained of syrup, they may be used as a jam to top crumpets or scones, or to flavour ice cream. They are the superior choice for crumbles and cobblers, because the fruit is evenly sweet and some of its liquid has already been drawn out, preventing a too-juicy pudding. Ohio plum farmer Eliphas Cope writes:

> A very rich preserve may be made [...] from the Damson. [...] In canning, the fruit should be sweetened to taste when put up, the fruit boiled in the syrup, as many have ignorantly condemned the cooked plum by presuming that sugar cast in the dish will suit to the taste this most wholesome and desirable fruit. The tartness of the plum requires that it be met to the seed with the sweet.[8]

A superficial strewing of sugar onto a dish of cooked damsons will not adequately sweeten them. Cooking and storing damsons in a syrup permits the sugar to pervade the flesh all the way to the stone, evenly imbuing the fruit with a sweetness that beautifully showcases its characteristic astringency. Preserving damsons whole, in the styles described below, ensures that the sweet will meet the seed.

EARLY AMERICAN DAMSON PRESERVE

This recipe for damson preserves comes from America's first cookbook, *American Cookery*. The mysterious author, Amelia Simmons, self-identifies as 'an American orphan', and nothing more is conclusively known about her. Simmons offers an orange and brandy-spiked damson preserve in her second edition (1796). She doesn't specify a quantity of damsons, but a review of her other preserve recipes suggests that three to four pounds would be appropriate for the quantity of sugar indicated. Karen Hess, editor of Applewood Books' facsimile edition of *American Cookery*, describes damsons as 'an exceptionally fine preserving plum [...], long popular in England, now very difficult to find'.[9] After using the preserved damsons in a crumble or cake, try adding the leftover syrup and a splash of sparkling water to red wine for a quick sangria.

> Take 4 pound of sugar and 1 quart of water, boil and scum clean, then run thro' a jelly bag, to which add one fresh orange cut fine, and half pint of brandy; to this syrrup put the damsons, let them do over a gentle fire 15 minutes; put away for use. Cherries and grapes may be preserved in the same way.[10]

'To Preserve Damsons' as the Wordsworths did

This recipe comes from the Wordsworth household; Dove Cottage in Grasmere is close to the damson-growing areas of the Lake District. Culinary historian Peter Brears adapted the original recipe to modern use by filling screw-top jam jars with damsons, covering them with sugar, and baking the open jars on a tray at 150 C / 300 F for a half hour. For large damsons, I recommend permitting the jars to cool, then baking a second time for 15 minutes. While this preserve will only improve as the damsons rest in their syrup, I have made it in the morning and used it in a crumble later the same day with success. Brears describes the result as 'the most succulent luscious and richly flavoured of all preserves'.[11]

> To one pt of Damsons, put 6 oz of Sugar, tie the bottles over with bladders & bake after the bread is drawn.

'A Very Nice Preserve of Damsons'

This recipe from Mrs Beeton presents the task of cooking damsons to softness without breaking the skins. My several attempts have been aesthetic failures in this regard, but the preserve tastes great. This recipe should be made with one part granulated sugar to four parts damsons.

Put the damsons (which should be picked from the stalks and quite free from blemishes) into a jar, with pounded sugar sprinkled amongst them in the above proportion; tie the jar closely down, set it in a saucepan of cold water; bring it gradually to boil, and simmer gently until the damsons are soft, without being broken. Let them stand till cold; then strain the juice from them, boil it up well, strain it through a jelly-bag, and pour it over the fruit. Let it cool, cover with oiled papers, and the jars with tissue-paper brushed over on both sides with the white of an egg, and store away in a dry cool place.

PICKLED DAMSONS

Pickled damsons are a pleasant and unexpected accompaniment to soft cheeses such as creamy Lancashire. This early twentieth century recipe from Margaret Alice Fairclough yields preserved fruits ideal for entertaining or gift-giving. If at first the liquid does not appear to cover the damsons, wait a few minutes. The firm damsons will soften and sink down as they warm up. In the final stage, I recommend gentle heating rather than boiling.

500 g / 1 lb damsons
225 g / 7 ½ oz granulated sugar
150 ml / 5 fl oz / ⅔ cup vinegar
8 whole cloves
5 cm / 2 in cinnamon stick

Wipe the damsons dry, and prick them all over with a needle. Put the damsons into jars; boil the vinegar with the sugar, and pour it boiling over the damsons. Let them stand for twenty-four hours, then heat up the vinegar again and let it stand twenty-four hours more. After that, boil the damsons, vinegar, and spices together, but do not break the skins. Fill up the jars, tie down, and they are fit for use in six weeks.

Pickled Damsons with Lemon and Ginger

This recipe follows a similar process to the one above. Either recipe may be doubled/halved, and larger batches may be heat-processed for long-term storage. Because of their bright citrus and spice profile, these pickled damsons are especially suited to wintertime feasts, cheese boards, or appetizer trays. After the final heating, you may find that the softened damsons and syrup can be packed in smaller/ fewer jars. If excess syrup remains, add it to sparkling water for a refreshing spiced damson lemonade.

500 g / 1 lb fresh, ripe damsons
225 g / 7 ½ oz sugar
150 ml / 5 fl oz / ⅔ cup fresh squeezed lemon juice
8 whole cloves
½ whole star anise
5 cm / 2 in cinnamon stick (Ceylon preferred)
80 g / 3 oz fresh ginger root, peeled and diced

Wash, dry, and prick the fresh damsons (approximately ten times each). Place the damsons in spotless jars that have been dried 10-15 minutes in a 110 C / 230 F oven. Bring the sugar and lemon juice just to the boil, stirring to ensure sugar is dissolved. Pour the hot liquid over the damsons, evenly distributing the liquid between jars (the liquid may seem too little at first, but there is no need to make more). Cover with a tea towel and let stand for 24 hours. Strain off the liquid, heat it to boiling again, and pour back over the damsons. Let stand for 24 hours as before. The next day, boil the liquid again, this time including the spices. Pour over the damsons one last time. Affix lids and allow to rest in the refrigerator, or a cool, dark cupboard for at least six weeks before tasting.

DAMSON CHEESES

For centuries the English have been making fruit into stiff pastes that condense its rich essence and preserve its vivid flavour. Pastes eventually came to be called 'cheeses': a 1780 christening dinner in Norfolk, attended by the Reverend James Woodforde, concluded with 'a good Desert of Fruit [...] amongst which was a Damson Cheese'.[12] The sliceable stiffness of damson cheese is comparable to that of *membrillo* (Spanish quince paste), firmer than an American jellied cranberry sauce, but pulpier than a gumdrop. Damson cheese may be served as a condiment for hot or cold meat entrees, dusted with icing sugar as a sweet, or nestled among selections on the cheese board. Stiltons and creamy young farm cheeses are frequently paired with damson cheese, but cheddars and Bries are wonderful too. Medicinally, a sliver of fruit cheese placed on a patient's tongue relieves dry mouth during the night, without the potential risks of liquid refreshment.

In its most basic form, damson cheese contains only damsons and sugar. The texture is slightly grainy, resounding with a rich puckery plum flavour. Described by D. Hughson, author of *The Family Receipt-Book* (1817) as 'very agreeable [...] easily and by no means expensively prepared,' damson cheese is made by cooking damsons with a little water until they soften to mush, sieving, cooking the strained pulp further to evaporate excess liquid, and sweetening with sugar. Ratios of pulp to sugar vary: most indicate half the weight of the damson pulp in sugar, while others rely on a noncommittal 'to taste' measurement. Apples, other plums, or aromatics may be incorporated to complement the flavour of the damsons.

Patience is a crucial ingredient that ought to be listed with damsons and sugar. The pulp may need to cook on a low temperature with frequent stirring for up to four hours, depending on the size of the batch. To minimize cooking time, I strain off any thin juice from the cooked damsons and set aside for another use before rubbing the pulp through the sieve. (The juice can be used for Eliza Acton's damson solid, or a damson jelly.) The thicker the pulp when you start, the less time you'll wait for excess moisture to evaporate. Small batches will cook more quickly than large ones. A kilogram of damsons will make an appropriate quantity of cheese for a holiday dinner, and you won't spend your youth tending a pan of pulp. If the mixture gets too hot after the sugar is added, it is possible to end up with a stiff, chewy, gumdrop-like candy instead of a firm yet sliceable paste. If you desire lovely, gelatin-free damson gumdrops, do this on purpose with one of the higher sugar recipes, cook until glossy and thick, then quickly transfer to lightly oiled silicone moulds to cool. The mixture will become stubbornly stiff and sticky as it cools, so do not disturb it once cooling has begun. Unmould when cool and roll in granulated sugar to prevent the sweets from adhering to each other.

As moisture evaporates, the pulp must be tended carefully to prevent it catching, which will ruin the flavour of the batch. Frederick Nutt (1807) indicates that damson cheese is done when it is 'as stiff as you can possibly stir it', but other signs to look for are a mixture that drops in thick, jagged dollops off a spoon (rather than in dribbles or drips), that leaves a lingering channel when a spoon is dragged along the bottom of the pan, and that sets stiffly when a sample is cooled on a plate. If you find yourself short on time (or patience!) waiting for damson cheese to cook, you can always stop cooking the pulp early and use it as a spread or sauce. If you plan to shape the cheese in a mould, it must be quite stiff; to serve in a dish, a softer paste is acceptable. On a number of occasions, I have paused in the midst of cooking damson cheese, removed it from the heat, covered the pan, and returned a few hours later to continue the process, with no ill effects.

Damson cheese may be decanted into jars for storage, as with jam. Choose a shallow jar with straight or flared sides if you plan to turn it out onto a cheese board for serving. In a number of historic recipes, 'brandy papers' are prescribed to seal the cheese. For this method, writing paper or kitchen paper is cut into circles the size of the jar's opening, dipped in brandy, and pressed onto the surface of the cheese to prevent the formation of mould. In other iterations, the papers are brushed with whiskey or butter. Brandy papers may be used for short-term storage in the refrigerator, but heat-processing jars in a boiling water bath is an appropriate modern-day alternative for long-term storage. I find that most damson cheeses become firmer and easier to unmould after a ripening period of several months in their jars.

To make sumptuous sweets, pour hot damson cheese onto parchment or greaseproof paper, cut into shapes when set, and dust with icing sugar before serving. Theodore Garrett includes an ambitious recipe for 'Candied Knots of Damson Paste' in his *Encyclopaedia of Practical Cookery* (1892): sieved damson pulp is cooked with sugar to the ball stage, spread ⅛ in thick on a tin sheet, dried on both sides, cooled, cut into ½ inch strips, and fashioned into knots and figure-of-eights, before being dried further.

The recipes herein present a variety of options. All will lend a bright flavour and beautiful colour to the table.

Bullace Cheese (1700s)

May Byron's 1915 edition of *Pot-luck, or The British Home Cookery Book* includes this unattributed eighteenth-century recipe for bullace cheese. This early recipe relies on foraged hedgerow fruits, rather than cultivated damsons.

> Take your bullaces when they are full ripe, and to every quart of fruit put a quarter of a pound of loaf sugar beaten small. Put them in a jar in moderate oven to bake till they are soft, then rub them through a hair sieve, and to every pound of pulp, add half a pound of loaf sugar crushed fine. Then boil it four and a half hours over a slow fire, and keep stirring it all the time. Put it into pots, and tie brandy papers over them, and keep them in a dry place. When it has stood a few months, it will cut out very bright and fine. You may make sloe cheese the same way.

Frederick Nutt's Damson Cheese (1807)

Frederick Nutt flavours his 1807 damson cheese with *noyaux*, the bitter almond-scented kernels found within damson stones. He notes that this recipe is appropriate for bullaces and other plums as well.

Pick the damsons free from stalks, leaves, &c. put them into a jar, tie white paper over them, bake them in a slow oven till quite soft, rub them through a cullender while hot, put the pulp and juice which has passed through the cullender into a stew-pan with fine powdered sugar to your taste, boil it over a moderate fire till it is as stiff as you can possibly stir it, which will take three hours; keep stirring it to prevent it burning to the pan, and a few minutes before you take it off the fire put the kernels of the damsons into the pan, and mix with it, put it into cups or moulds, let it stand a day, and cut some pieces of writing paper the size of the tops of the cups or moulds, dip them in brandy and put close over them; put them in a dry place and they will keep for several years. [... It] is necessary to take the skins off the kernels before you put them into the pan.

Eliza Acton's 'Excellent' Damson Cheese (1845)

To prepare the fruit for this recipe, 'bake separately in a very slow oven [...] any number of fine ripe damsons, and one third the quantity of bullaces, or of any other pale plums, as a portion of their juice will, to most tastes, improve, by softening the flavour of the preserve, and will render the colour brighter'. To do this, bake the fruit at 120 C / 250 F for approximately 40 minutes.

When the fruit has been baked or stewed tender [...] drain off the juice, skin and stone the damsons, pour back to them from a third to half of their juice, weigh, and then boil them over a clear brisk fire until they form a quite dry paste; add six ounces of pounded sugar for each pound of the plums; stir them off the fire until this is dissolved, and boil the preserves again without quitting or ceasing to stir it, until it leaves the pan quite dry, and adheres in a mass to the spoon. If it should not stick to the fingers when lightly touched, it should be sufficiently done to keep very long; press it quickly into pans or moulds; lay on it a paper dipped in spirit when it is perfectly cold; tie another fold over it, and store it in a dry place. Bullace cheese is made in the same manner, and almost any kind of plum will make an agreeable preserve of the sort.

'DAMSON SOLID'

Eliza Acton's recipe for Damson Solid takes advantage of the naturally high pectin content of damsons and apples to create an attractive, cheese-like condiment. Apples mellow the tartness of damsons without dulling the magnificent colour the damsons impart. To speed the process of rendering damson juice, spread the fruit in a single layer on a parchment-lined, rimmed baking sheet, and bake at 190 C / 375 F for about 30 minutes, then drain off juice as indicated. The unused pulp may be sieved for use in sauces or damson cheese.

Pour juice from some damsons which have stood for a night in a very cool oven, or been stewed in a jar placed in a pan of water; weigh and put it into a preserving pan with a pound and four ounces of pearmains (or of any other fine boiling apples), pared, cored, and quartered, to each pound of the juice; boil these together, keeping them well stirred, from twenty-five to thirty minutes, then add the sugar [140z], and when it is nearly dissolved, continue the boiling for ten minutes. This, if done with exactness, will give a perfectly smooth and firm preserve, which may be moulded in small shapes, and turned out for table.

MRS BEETON'S DAMSON CHEESE (1861)

Mrs Beeton prescribes a half pound of sugar for each pound of cooked damson pulp. She notes a minimum of 1 pint of damsons is required to make 'a very small pot of cheese'.

Pick the stalks from the damsons, and put them into a preserving-pan; simmer them over the fire until they are soft, occasionally stirring them; then beat them through a coarse sieve, and put the pulp and juice into the preserving-pan, with sugar in the above proportion, having previously carefully weighed them. Stir the sugar well in, and simmer the damsons slowly for 2 hours. Skim well; then boil the preserve quickly for ½ hour, or until it looks firm and hard in the spoon; put it quickly into shallow pots, or very tiny earthenware moulds, and, when cold, cover it with oiled papers, and the jars with tissue-paper brushed over on both sides with the white of an egg. A few of the stones may be cracked, and the kernels boiled with the damsons, which very much improves the flavour of the cheese.

Festive Damson Apple Cheese with Orange and Spices

This bright, spiced damson cheese is the perfect alternative to cranberry sauce at holiday feasts. Previously frozen and thawed damsons will give up their stones more easily than fresh. Whether using fresh or frozen, be sure all stones are removed prior to cooking, in anticipation of the blending stage. This cheese is a bit sticky and is best served from a dish, within three months of being made.

6 wide ribbons of orange peel
350 g / 12 oz damsons, weighed after stones removed
350 g / 12 oz tart apple, peeled, cored, and chopped small before weighing
300 g / 10 oz granulated or caster sugar
pinch salt
pinch freshly grated nutmeg

1 allspice berry, ⅓ whole star anise, 5 cm / 2 in cinnamon stick,
and 2 cloves, lightly bashed and contained in a muslin sachet or
metal tea infuser

Combine the ingredients in a heavy pan and bring to a simmer
over medium heat. Stir periodically, mashing fruit with the back
of the spoon as it softens. After about 10 minutes, the fruit will
have broken down. Cool slightly, remove spice bundle, and
transfer to a blender or food processor. Blitz thoroughly. Wash
the pan. Rub the mixture through a fine-mesh sieve, into the
clean pan. Discard remaining pulp. Cook on medium-low or low
heat for about an hour, stirring frequently, until mixture thickens
to a stiff paste.

DAMSON TARTS, CAKES, AND OTHER BAKES

TARTS

Damson tarts are the stars of the 1868 play, *The Historie of the Knave*
of Hearts and the Damson Tarts. A romp of puns, politics, and pastry,
the play follows the exploits of the King and Queen of Hearts, who
decide to host a party for their royal friends. The naughty Knave of
Hearts steals to the kitchen and devours the Queen's damson tarts.
The Knave's crime is discovered and the King exclaims: 'His lips retain
the purple stain / Of juice upon them yet; / To hide his sin his mouth
and chin / To wipe he did forget.'

What follows here is an array of damson tart variations for your
cherished guests. Just don't leave anyone alone with them in the
kitchen.

A minimalist recipe for damson tart from Richard Dolby's *The*
Cook's Dictionary (1830) reads, 'Damson Tart: Make a nice crust, line
your dish, put in the fruit, and finish the same as for any other fruit
pie.' Well, that's sorted. If you prefer recipes with actual instructions,
read on…

SIXTEENTH-CENTURY DAMSON TART

A Proper Newe Booke of Cokerye (1575) features a saffron-tinted pastry for tarts. Alongside fillings of 'marygoldes, prim roses and Cowslips' we find a wine-infused, custardy damson filling:

> To make short paest for tarte.
> Take fyne floure and a cursey of fayre water and a dyshe of swete butter and a lyttel saffron, and the yolckes of two egges and make it thynne and as tender as ye maye.
> To make a tarte of damsons.
> Take Damsons and boyle them in wine, eyther red or claret, and put therto a dosin of peares, or els white bread to make them stuffe withall, then drain them up with the yolkes of six Egges, and sweet butter, and so bake it.

THOMAS DAWSON'S DAMSON TART

The damson tart from *The Good Huswifes Jewell* (1596) relies on a pre-baked pastry case and sweetened damson filling enriched with wine and spices:

> To make a Tarte of Damsons. Take Damsons and seeth them in Wine, and straine them with a little Creame, then yoyle your stuffe ouer the fire till it be thicke, put thereto, suger, synamon and ginger, but set it not into the Ouen after, but let your paste be baked before.[14]

MRS BEETON'S DAMSON TART

Mrs Beeton's simple damson tart is essentially stewed, sugared damsons under a lid made of short or puff pastry. Two of her shortcrust pastry recipes follow. A novel variation on this from the 1920s called Damson and Banana Pie is reprinted by Victoria Barratt in her *A Taste of Damsons* booklet (1997). Damsons and sugar are layered with peeled, sliced bananas, covered with pastry and baked in the same manner as the tart below.

1 ¼ pints of damsons
¼ lb of moist sugar
½ lb of short or puff crust

Put the damsons, with the sugar between them, into a deep pie-dish, in the midst of which, place a small cup or jar turned upside down; pile the fruit high in the middle, line the edges of the dish with short or puff crust, whichever may be preferred; put on the cover, ornament the edges, and bake from ½ to ¾ hour in a good oven. If puff-crust is used, about 10 minutes before the pie is done, take it out of the oven, brush it over with the white of an egg beaten to a froth with the blade of a knife; strew some sifted sugar over, and a few drops of water, and put the tart back to finish baking: with short crust, a little plain sifted sugar, sprinkled over, is all that will be required.

Mrs Beeton offers two shortcrust pastry options, one without eggs, and one with:

'Very Good Short Crust for Fruit Tarts'

To every lb of flour allow ¾ lb of butter, 1 tablespoonful of sifted sugar, ⅓ pint of water. Rub the butter into the flour, after having ascertained that the latter is perfectly dry; add the sugar, and mix the whole into a stiff paste, with about ⅓ pint of water. Roll it out two or three times, folding the paste over each time, and it will be ready for use.

'Another Good Short Crust'

To every lb of flour allow 8 oz of butter, the yolks of 2 eggs,

2 oz of sifted sugar, about ¼ pint of milk. Rub the butter into the flour, add the sugar, and mix the whole as lightly as possible to a smooth paste, with the yolks of eggs well beaten, and the milk. The proportion of the latter ingredient must be judged of by the size of the eggs: if these are large, so much will not be required, and more if the eggs are smaller.

DAMSON MERINGUE TART

This recipe for 'Damson Flan' appeared in the 3 October 1938 edition of the *Manchester Guardian*. Tart pulp and mellow meringue balance each other in a sturdy crust. Dock the pastry by pricking with a fork before adding the weights to ensure a flat bottom. Bake at 200 C / 400 F for 15 minutes, remove weights, and bake a further 5 minutes. I recommend whisking a tablespoon of arrowroot starch or another thickening agent into the pulp and returning to the heat in a clean pan to cook further if the filling seems too loose. To avoid lumps, thoroughly dissolve the starch in a few tablespoons of pulp separately, then incorporate. Depending on the size of your eggs, two might be necessary for the topping. Double the sugar accordingly. To crisp the meringue, set oven to 90 C / 200 F.

Make some short pastry with half a pound of flour, a pinch of salt, four ounces of butter or margarine, the yolk of an egg, a little water, and a level tablespoonful of castor sugar. Roll out and line a flan case or sandwich tin with it. Cover with greaseproof paper and weigh down with peas or beans. Bake in a hot oven until golden brown, then remove paper and peas and let the bottom dry out in the oven. Slip out of the case and leave to cool. While it is baking put a pound of damsons in a pan with about four ounces of sugar and stew until soft, then rub the pulp through a coarse sieve. Spread this on the pastry when cool. Whisk the white of the egg to a stiff froth and fold in a dessertspoonful of castor sugar. Put on top of the fruit and put in a cool oven for a few minutes to crisp the meringue. Good hot or cold.

Rustic Damson Tart

This rustic tart has been my go-to for years because it always seems to work, even on a humid summer's day. The damsons retain their defining juicy astringency, contrasted with crumbly, sugar-crusted pastry. Other stone fruits, or even thinly sliced mango, may be used for a change. The rustic structure is forgiving and sturdy enough to be toted off on a picnic. It is best served at room temperature (not hot from the oven). Any leftovers may be savoured, cold from the refrigerator, for breakfast the next morning. This is an unfussy tart for living life to the fullest.

Pastry
180 g / 6 oz plain flour
2 tablespoons caster sugar
¼ teaspoon salt
110 g / 3 ½ oz unsalted butter
approx 50 ml / 1 ¾ fl oz / ¼ cup cold vodka (or water)

Filling
500 g / 1 lb damsons (you may require less)
6 tablespoons granulated sugar, divided into 4, 1, and 1 tablespoon
½ teaspoon ground ginger
¼ teaspoon ground cinnamon
1 tablespoon plain flour
1 egg, beaten, or a few tablespoons milk to brush on the pastry

4 tablespoons warmed fruit jelly of choice, for glazing the fruit after baking (optional)

To make the pastry: Combine flour, sugar, and salt. Rub in butter until the mixture resembles bread crumbs. Add cold vodka or water gradually, 1 tablespoon at a time, incorporating until moist clumps form. Gather into a ball, form a disk, wrap in cling film and refrigerate at least 1 hour.

To make the tart: Preheat oven to 200 C / 400 F. Wash, dry, and remove stones from damsons. Toss damsons, 4 of the 6 tablespoons of sugar, and spices in a bowl. Roll chilled dough into an approximate oval or round shape the thickness of a pound coin. Transfer to a parchment-lined, rimmed baking sheet. (No worries if pastry overlaps tray edges at this point.) Combine 1 tablespoon flour and 1 tablespoon sugar and sprinkle across the centre of the dough, leaving a generous 5 cm / 2 in margin on all sides. Distribute the damson pieces across the sprinkled centre of the pastry, maintaining the plain margin. If any liquid has gathered at the bottom of the bowl, omit it. The damsons should form a solid, single layer with no gaps. If you find you have more damsons than you need, set aside the extras for another use. Fold the pastry margins toward the centre, tucking as needed to create attractive, rustic folds around the perimeter of the tart. The plums should be completely encased at the edges, with no cracks or tears through which liquid may escape during baking. Brush the pastry with beaten egg or milk and sprinkle the entire tart with remaining tablespoon of sugar. Bake until plums are bubbly and crust is golden, about 45 minutes. Upon removing from oven, brush warmed jelly over the fruit to add shine.

CAKES

DAMSON-TOP SHORTCAKE

Damson jam gives this dense cake a magenta-swirled top. Serve intact or split to make a sandwich, with jam, ice cream, or custard, any of which the cake will greedily absorb. Best eaten the day it's baked, as it dries out quickly.

250 g / 8 oz self-raising flour

30 g / 1 oz granulated sugar
80 g / 3 oz cold, unsalted butter
250 ml / 8 fl oz / 1 cup milk
4 tablespoons prepared damson jam or jelly, warmed
Cream, ice cream, or custard for serving

Prepare a 20 cm / 8 in tin by rubbing with butter. Heat oven to 225 C / 450 F. Combine flour and sugar; rub in cold butter until mixture resembles coarse meal. Add milk and stir until just combined. Transfer to prepared tin. Check the warmed jam: its consistency should be slightly loose from being warmed, but not liquid. Drop spoonfuls of warm jam onto the batter. Run a knife or skewer through the jam blobs until the entire surface is covered in an even, attractive swirl pattern. Bake 15-20 minutes, until golden and firm. Cool for 5 minutes in the pan, then transfer to a rack to finish cooling. Once cool, wrap tightly in cling film until ready to serve to prevent the cake drying out. Alternatively, remove the still-warm cake and carefully split horizontally. Lightly butter the cut side of the bottom layer. Add more jam, and/or ice cream or custard. Position top layer and serve immediately.

DAMSON STREUSEL TRAYBAKE

This spiced traybake is perfect for breakfast time or alongside an afternoon cup of tea. Lashings of glaze help to balance the intensely tart, jammy pockets of damson embedded in the sweet, soft cake. Allow it to cool to room temperature before serving. It's a cake that gets better after a rest in the refrigerator. This recipe is based on an American 'coffee cake' my mother used to make, and, in the springtime, chopped fresh rhubarb in the same quantities can be swapped for damsons with appealing results.

Cake
400 g / 14 oz granulated sugar
2 eggs

1 teaspoon vanilla extract
160 g / 5 oz butter
350 g / 12 oz plain flour
1 teaspoon fine salt
2 teaspoon bicarbonate of soda
1 teaspoon cinnamon or mixed spice
1 kg / 2 lb damsons (chopped, stones removed)

Streusel
100 g / 3 ½ oz cold butter
100 g / 3 ½ oz soft light brown sugar
50 g / 1 ¾ oz plain flour

Icing
250 g / 8 oz icing sugar
2-3 tablespoons milk, heated
1 teaspoon vanilla extract

For the cake: Combine butter, sugar, eggs, and vanilla and beat until light and creamy. In a separate bowl, whisk together flour, salt, soda, and cinnamon. Add dry ingredients to wet and mix until just combined. (The mixture will be thick, almost paste-like; this ensures that the juicy damsons stay evenly distributed during baking.) Fold in the chopped damsons. Transfer to an oiled 33 x 22.3 cm / 13 x 9 in tin or baking dish. In the dry ingredients bowl, combine streusel ingredients, rubbing with fingertips until crumbly. Strew the streusel over the cake and bake at 180 C / 350 F for 45 minutes. As it bakes, whisk together the icing ingredients, adding hot milk and vanilla to the sugar gradually until it is the consistency of a smooth, thick-but-pourable sauce. Allow cake to cool to room temperature before drizzling generously with icing.

DAMSON CREAM CHEESE ICING

Give any cake a damson upgrade with a luxurious layer of sweet-tart pastel pink icing. Damson icing pairs well with dark gingerbread cakes, fudgy chocolate cakes, zesty citrus cakes and moist vanilla cakes. Any preserved damsons may be used: damson jam will fleck the buttercream with pulp, and damson jelly or butter will produce a uniform colour. If using whole preserved damsons or jam, remove stones and chop finely, sieve, or blitz in a food processor to minimize lumps in the icing. Six tablespoons of preserved damsons will give a light damson flavour. Amplify to taste by adding more. This recipe yields enough to generously ice the tops of two full-size loaf cakes or the middle and top of a round sandwich cake.

> *150 g / 5 oz unsalted butter, softened*
> *100 g / 3 ½ oz cream cheese or mascarpone, softened*
> *1 teaspoon vanilla*
> *450 g / 1 lb icing sugar*
> *at least 6 tablespoons damson jam, jelly, or butter (see note above)*

With an electric mixer, combine the softened butter, cream cheese, and vanilla. Add the icing sugar and beat on low speed until fully incorporated. Add the damson component of choice, mix to incorporate, then increase speed to high and whip a further 5 minutes until fluffy. (This final step is essential to achieve a light texture.) Spread or pipe swirls of damson buttercream onto cake. Refrigerate if not serving within a few hours.

OTHER BAKES

SIMPLE BAKED DAMSONS

Baking damsons whole with sugar yields a casserole of tender fruits and syrup that may be ladled luxuriously over ice cream. The intact stones slide effortlessly from the velvety baked damson flesh, and as long as guests have been forewarned, cracked teeth may be eschewed. This manner of preparing damsons was introduced to me by Helen Platt of Kendal, who characterizes this not as a recipe, but as 'throwing a few things in an oven without too much weighing and timing, and drinking some gin whilst they cook'. It is recommended to enjoy this dish as Mrs Platt and I do: with ice cream, reclining on settees, surrounded by cats.

Wash the damsons, removing stems and leaves. In a baking dish, layer damsons with approximately 250 g / 8 oz soft brown sugar per kilo of fruit. A sprinkle of ground ginger or cinnamon may be added if desired. Bake at 180 C / 350 F for 15-20 minutes, until damsons are completely soft and a syrup has formed around them. Remove from oven before skins split for the most attractive presentation.

DAMSON CRUMBLE

Served with ice cream, a crumble offers lush baked fruit and the soft crunch of sweet, fragrant streusel. Fresh damsons release a great deal of liquid when heated, resulting in a soupy mess rather than a dense fruity base. Using already preserved damsons means easier prep (open the jar, strain off the syrup, and the base is ready). Preserved damsons may be combined with sliced apples (toss them with a little of the damson syrup), other stone fruits, or berries. Recipes for Early American Preserves, Mrs Beeton's Very Nice Preserve of Damsons, and Lemon Pickled Damsons work well here. The leftover syrup can be added to seltzer, lemonade, prosecco, or fruit salad, or stored in the freezer for another use. It's the work of a few minutes to pick through the preserved damsons individually to remove the stones, and you'll have nothing to worry about when you serve the crumble.

1.5 kg / 3 lb preserved damsons
125 g / 4 oz plain flour
100 g / 3 ½ oz soft brown sugar
100 g / 3 ½ oz cold unsalted butter, cut into pieces
¼ teaspoon each ground cinnamon, nutmeg, and sea salt
handful of flaked almonds (add after blending other ingredients)

Drain the excess syrup from approximately 1.5 kg / 3 lb preserved damsons, remove stones, and spread evenly in a baking dish. Combine the streusel ingredients (except almonds) in a bowl that is wide and shallow enough to get your hands into. Rub the butter into the dry ingredients, until it is fully incorporated and the mixture forms crumbly clumps when squeezed. Add almonds and toss lightly to combine, breaking up any large clumps. Heat oven to 190 C / 375 F. Distribute the prepared streusel evenly across the damsons. Bake for 30-40 minutes until streusel is golden and juices are bubbling at the edges. Allow to cool to room temperature and serve with ice cream, whipped cream, or custard.

Scone-Topped Damson Apple Cobbler

Fluffy mounds of scone batter form a cakey lid atop a tart-sweet layer of apple slices and damson preserves. Use any of the preserve recipes recommended for crumble, in a ratio of 1-2 parts apples to 1 part damsons. The quantity of fruit needed will depend on the depth of your baking dish. It's vital to dollop the scone mixture onto hot fruit, leaving spaces between to permit expansion. Best served with pouring custard, which the topping will readily absorb.

15 g / ½ oz granulated sugar
175 g / 6 oz self-raising flour
50 g / 1 ¾ oz butter
1 egg
approximately 100 ml / 3 ½ fl oz / ½ cup milk, to top egg up to
150 ml / 5 fl oz / ⅔ cup
1 teaspoon lemon or lime juice
good baking apples, peeled, cored, and thinly sliced
damson preserves, drained, stones removed, syrup reserved
a few pinches ground cinnamon, allspice, or mixed spice

Heat oven to 200 C / 400 F. Combine apple slices and preserved damsons in a baking dish. Toss the fruit with the spices and a little of the reserved syrup. Transfer to the oven and bake for 15 minutes while you prepare the topping. Crack the egg into a measuring jug and top up with milk for a total of 150 ml / 5 fl oz / ⅔ cup of liquid. Add lemon juice, whisk to combine, and set aside. Combine flour and granulated sugar. Rub butter into flour to uniform, sandy consistency. Stir in the milk-egg mixture and let it rest until the fruit base is ready. The mixture will puff slightly as it rests. Remove the pre-baked fruit from the oven and drop scoops of batter onto hot fruit in equal-size portions, permitting a gap of 1-2 cm between dollops. Bake 20-25 minutes until scone topping is puffed, firm, and golden, with syrupy juices bubbling at the edges.

Damson and Rice Pudding

This easy pudding from Eliza Acton (1845) makes use of prepared damson jam for flavour and colour. Bake at 165 C / 325 F.

> With five ounces of whole rice boiled soft and dry, mix an ounce of butter, ten ounces of damson-jam, a teaspoonful of lemon-juice, and five eggs. Beat the whole well together, and bake it about half an hour.

Damson Puddings

Not bakes, but two variations on damson puddings.

A cloth-boiled pudding from Hannah Glasse (1774):

> Take a quart of milk, beat six eggs, half the whites, with half a pint of the milk and four spoonfuls of flour, a little fat, and two spoonfuls of beaten ginger; then by degrees mix in all the milk, and a pound of damsons, tie it in a cloth, boil it an hour, melt butter, and pour over it.

A basin-boiled pudding from Mrs Dalgairns (1829):

> Make a batter with three well-beaten eggs, a pint of milk, and of flour and brown sugar four table-spoonfuls each; stone a

pint of damsons, and mix them with the batter; boil it in a
buttered basin for an hour and a half.

Chilled Damson Desserts

Erbowle

This damson/bullace pudding recipe comes from the oldest known
English cookery text, *The Forme of Cury* (1390), which was written
for the master cooks of King Richard II and transcribed by Samuel
Pegge in 1780. Erbowle is a pudding made with 'bolas' (a medieval
spelling of bullace). The transcription and adaptation below come from
Pleyn Delit: Medieval Cookery for Modern Cooks, by Constance Hieatt,
Brenda Hosington, and Sharon Butler.[15] When made with damsons, this
pudding is tart and gently set, with an almost mousse-like lightness. If
you're not put off by anachronism, wait until it is set and layer it, parfait
style, in tall clear glasses, with the 1808 Damson Froth that follows.

Take bolas and scald hem with wyne and drawe hem þorow a
straynour; do hem in a pot. Clarify hony, and do þerto with
powdour fort and flour of rys. Salt it & florissh it with whyte
aneys & serve it forth.

The authors translate and modernize this dish for plums, but damsons
work well in it:

Fresh Plum Pudding

1 lb ripe fresh plums
1 cup each red wine, water
¼ cup clear honey
¼ teaspoon each salt, cinnamon
⅛ teaspoon each galingale or ginger, mace
¼ cup rice flour, stirred into ¼ cup cold water

Put plums in a saucepan and cover with wine and water; bring to a boil and simmer 5 minutes. Remove plums; peel them and discard pits. Blend them with honey and spices; stir this puréed mixture back into the cooking liquid in the pan. Carefully stir in rice flour mixture and blend thoroughly, stirring over medium heat about 7-8 minutes, until the pudding is quite thick. If there are any lumps, reblend (or strain). Pour into a serving bowl, and when it is cool, chill. If you have any candied anise seed, scatter it over the top when the pudding has set.

Damson Froth to Set on Cream, Custard, or Trifle

The damson reaches new heights in this intriguing 1808 pudding topping from 'A Lady', the pseudonym of Shropshire's Maria Eliza Rundell. Rundell assembled the manuscript that would become *Domestic Cookery* for use by her daughters, addressing her instructions to the mistress of the house, rather than the servants. From her humble beginnings in Ludlow, Mrs Rundell acquired a small fortune from her bestselling book, the precursor to domestic manuals published throughout the nineteenth century.[16] Here, damson pulp is whipped with beaten egg whites and sculpted into peaks atop a trifle or custard. You may sweeten the pulp to taste, but a quarter pound sugar to the half pound pulp is a good place to start, and a few drops of vanilla extract make a nice addition. To prepare the pulp, cook 500 g / 1 lb whole damsons with 50 ml / 1 ¾ fl oz / ¼ cup water until soft, then sieve out the skins and stones. This will yield approximately 250 ml / 8 fl oz / 1 cup of pulp. Whip the egg whites to soft peaks before adding the pulp, a few spoonfuls at a time and in rapid succession, so that their integration coincides with the stiff peak stage, and the mixture does not break from overbeating. I was skeptical that this would stand 'as high as you choose' but it does indeed fluff up impressively. This recipe appears without attribution throughout the nineteenth and twentieth centuries, but Mrs Rundell's was the earliest version I encountered.

Sweeten half a pound of the pulp of damsons, or any other sort of scalded fruit; put to it the whites of four eggs beaten, and beat the pulp with them till it will stand as high as you choose, and being put on the cream, &c. with a spoon, it will take any form; it should be rough, to imitate a rock.

One might serve Damson Froth layered anachronistically with medieval Erbowle, or, atop 'Floating Island', as suggested in *Cassell's Dictionary of Cookery* (1883). To make the base: 'Into three-quarters of a pint of cream put sugar to make it very sweet, and the juice and rind of a lemon grated. Beat it for ten minutes. Cut French rolls into thin slices, and lay them on a round dish on the top of the cream. On this put a layer of apricot or currant jam, and some more slices of roll. Pile up on this, very high, a whip made of damson jam, and the whites of four eggs. [...] Garnish with fruit or sweetmeats.'

DAMSON ETON MESS

Super-tart damsons meet luscious cream with a crunch of sugary meringue in this version of the classic. To up the kitsch, channel a mid-century 'whip' style dessert by foregoing meringues and folding in chopped walnuts, shredded sweetened coconut, and mini marshmallows.

500 g / 1 lb damsons
50 g / 1 ¾ oz granulated sugar
dash of ground anise seed

500 ml / ⅞ pint double cream
4 tablespoons caster or icing sugar
meringues (shop-bought or home-made)

Combine damsons, sugar, and anise seed over medium heat with a splash of water and cook until soft and pulpy (10-15 minutes). Rub the pulp through a fine sieve to remove stones and skins. Set aside to cool completely. Whip double cream to stiff peaks, add caster or icing sugar. Crumble half the meringues on top of the cream, and add about two-thirds of the damson purée. Fold gently , leaving large streaks. Layer into dishes with additional crumbled meringue and lashings of damson purée. Serve immediately.

WENSLEYDALE CHEESECAKE WITH DAMSON COULIS

In Hawes, Yorkshire, the Wensleydale Creamery cafe's 'Ultimate Wensleydale Cheese Experience' concludes with a slice of Wensleydale cheesecake studded with spicy nuggets of stem ginger. This easy cheesecake can be made in a springform pan, or as bite-size minis for a party. I've adapted the Creamery's recipe slightly and topped it with a tart damson coulis. You may wish to halve or quarter this recipe. A small portion is quite satisfying.

For the base
225 g / 7 ½ oz digestive biscuits, crushed
85 g / 3 oz butter

For the filling
500 g / 1 lb Wensleydale cheese, crumbled
500 g / 1 lb cream cheese, softened
2-3 tablespoons cream
85 g / 3 oz stem ginger, diced (optional)
2-3 tablespoons icing sugar

For the Damson Coulis as topping (see following recipe)

To prepare the base, mix crushed biscuits with melted butter and press into a 20 cm / 8 in springform tin. Refrigerate while preparing the filling.

To prepare the filling, mix cheeses (an electric mixer works best), add some cream to loosen (but keep the mixture fairly stiff). Add ginger and icing sugar. Top the biscuit base the with mixture, smooth the top, and chill thoroughly.

For bite-size mini cheesecakes, line a mini muffin tray with paper cases. Tamp one teaspoon of crumb crust into each. Top with a tablespoon of filling. When all are filled, tap the tray on the work surface to level the cheesecake mixture. Chill until set, in the tray. The structure of the tray is needed to help the filling hold its shape until the cheesecakes become firm.

Delicious cold or at room temperature, but best somewhere in between – about 30 minutes out of the refrigerator. Serve plated cheesecake slices topped with damson coulis, or, for mini cheesecakes, adorn individually with coulis and swirl into the cheese filling with a skewer before refrigerating.

DAMSON COULIS

An elegant finish for cheesecake and ice cream.

500 g / 1 lb damsons
150 ml / 5 fl oz / ⅔ cup water
150 g / 5 oz granulated or caster sugar
2 tablespoons lemon juice

Simmer damsons in water, stirring occasionally, until the fruit is soft. Rub through a sieve to remove skins and stones. Wipe out the pan. Return the sieved damson pulp to the pan along with the lemon juice, and reduce over a medium heat until the desired consistency is achieved. Add sugar and stir until dissolved. Cool thoroughly.

DAMSON FIZZ JELLY

This sparkling jewel-toned jelly makes a light, palate-cleansing finish in warm or cool weather. To make damson juice: bake damsons at 180 C / 350 F until they release their juice. This may take up to 30 minutes for large damsons, and longer if they are frozen. Alternatively, place the damsons in an electric pressure cooker with ¼ cup water. Process at high pressure for 6 minutes. Allow to release naturally for 15 minutes. Drain off the juice from the cooked damsons then place them in a sieve to drip for a further 30 minutes. To maintain the clarity of the juice, do not press through the sieve. (The remaining pulp may be used for a sauce or a damson cheese.) A kilo of damsons should yield about 250 ml / 8 fl oz / 1 cup of juice. If the yield is slightly less, top up with water or wine. You may replace prosecco with a fruity red wine in this recipe for a less sweet, more intense jelly.

Sprinkle one ounce of unflavoured gelatin powder over 250 ml / 8 fl oz / 1 cup of cold water and let it stand 5 minutes to soften. Over a low heat, warm until the gelatin dissolves completely, 3 minutes. Add 100 g / 3 ½ oz granulated sugar and stir a few minutes until completely dissolved. Combine with 500 ml / ⅞ pint damson juice and 500 ml / ⅞ pint prosecco in a mixing bowl and stir gently. Transfer to individual serving dishes, skim the foam, and chill until firm (about 4 hours). May be made a day in advance. Serves six.

Damson Ice Cream (1807)

This minimalist recipe for damson ice cream comes from the expanded 1807 edition of Frederick Nutt's *The Complete Confectioner*, originally published in 1789. This recipe tastes more of lemon than of damson, but the damsons give it a fine pale pink colour. Made with double cream, it freezes quickly and the finished product has a crumbly texture that melts to soft foam. Compared to today's ice creams, it does not taste very sweet, but it pairs nicely with a sweet cake.

> Take three ounces of preserved damsons, pound them and break the stones of them, put them into a bason, squeeze in two lemons, and a pint of cream; press them through a sieve, and freeze it.

Damson Ice Cream (1817)

Nutt relied on preserved damsons; this recipe from Joseph Bell's *Treatise on Confectionary* is made with fresh fruit. Ivan Day, a food scholar well known for his recreations of historic recipes, recommended this recipe, which he described as 'spectacular'.

Put damsons into a stone jar; cover them, and set them in a slow oven; when dissolved, pulp them through a hair sieve; to one pound of pulp, add twelve ounces of sifted loaf sugar; to which, mix in, when cold, one quart of cream, and freeze.

Damson Swirl Ice Cream

This recipe is adapted from the base developed by Jeni Britton Bauer, proprietor of ice cream parlours across the midwestern United States and author of two bestselling ice cream books. The resulting ice cream is thick, smooth, and luxurious. To ensure successful freezing, make the base a day ahead and chill overnight before churning in your ice cream maker. If you already have some sweetened damson purée in your freezer, use that and skip the first step.

For the damson swirl
500 g / 1 lb damsons
50 g / 1 ¾ oz granulated sugar

For the ice cream base
400 ml / 14 fl oz full fat milk
2 tablespoons tapioca starch or cornflour (cornstarch in the US)
30 g / 1 oz cream cheese, softened
generous pinch fine salt
400 ml / 14 fl oz double cream
130 g / 4 oz granulated sugar
2 tablespoons golden syrup
1 whole star anise (optional, but very nice)

To prepare the damson swirl: Heat the oven to 190 C / 375 F. Cut the damsons in half, remove the stones, and spread the fruit across a rimmed baking sheet, lined with parchment. Toss with granulated sugar. Roast for 15 minutes, stirring any unincorporated sugar into the juices at the midpoint. The damsons are done when they are soft and juicy, surrounded by syrup. Remove from the oven and cool completely. In a blender or food processor, purée the cooked plums and syrup until only tiny flecks remain. Refrigerate.

To prepare the base: In a small cup, combine two tablespoons of the milk with the cornflour. In a large bowl (the vessel in which you intend to chill the mixture overnight), whisk the salt and the softened cream cheese. In a heavy, medium saucepan, combine cream, golden syrup, sugar, and the remaining milk. Boil briskly for 4 minutes. Remove from the heat and whisk in the corn flour mixture. Return to the boil for one minute, stirring constantly as it thickens. Add the hot milk mixture to the cream cheese gradually, whisking to ensure the cream cheese melts completely. Once all the hot milk is added, mix in 125 ml / 4 fl oz / ½ cup of the damson purée. You may wish to dip the bowl of hot mixture into a larger bowl containing ice and water to speed cooling. Cover and refrigerate the mixture overnight. The pectin in the damson purée will further thicken the mixture as it cools. The next day, churn according to your ice cream maker instructions.

While the ice cream is churning, prepare a loaf tin or other container. Line the tin with cling film, with two pieces layered perpendicularly, end to end and side to side. Allow ample overhang. Scoop one-third of the churned ice cream into the prepared container. Working quickly, swirl a few tablespoons of the remaining purée over the surface. Repeat with two more layers of ice cream, finishing with an attractive purée swirl on top. Fold the cling film overhangs across the ice cream, pressing it smooth against the surface to prevent a skin or frost from forming. Freeze until firm, at least several hours. To serve, lift the wrapped parcel out of the tin and cut into slices or cubes to show off the swirl. (Alternatively, layer the ice cream and damson purée in any airtight container, press cling film to the surface, and scoop to serve.)

DAMSON SORBET

Chef Yannick Lequitte, educator at Kendal College, presented this recipe at a Damson Day cookery demonstration in the Lyth Valley. Prepare a purée by cooking 1 kg / 2 lb damsons (stones removed) with 250 g / 8 oz of sugar, a little water and 2 tablespoons lemon juice. Cook the fruit until very soft and blend to achieve a purée. Create a syrup by bringing 1 litre / 1 ¾ pints of water and 675 g / 1 ½ lb of sugar to the boil. Mix equal quantities of the purée and the syrup. Add sorbet stabiliser at a ratio of 1 teaspoon of per 1000 g of base to improve the texture of the sorbet. Using an ice cream maker, churn the cooled mixture until you have achieved the desired consistency. Freeze.

DAMSON SAUCES AND CONDIMENTS

The sharp acidity of damsons makes them an appropriate condiment for any meat dish, from game to poultry, as well as for simple cheese sandwiches. These recipes make manageable-sized batches for use within a few weeks to a month. To preserve surplus low-sugar sauces for a later meal, decant by the tablespoon into ice cube trays, freeze, and then release sauce cubes into a freezer bag, pressing to remove excess air before sealing. High-sugar sauces (such as the barbecue sauce) don't freeze entirely solid, so storage of leftovers in a freezer bag or jar works best. Thaw the frozen sauces gently in a microwave or saucepan, whisking to remedy any separation that has occurred. For best results, use frozen sauces within six months.

JAMMY DAMSON TOMATO SANDWICH SPREAD

A cross between a jam and a relish, this dynamic spread is excellent with cream cheese or goat's cheese on crackers, or on cheddar sandwiches. Try using it to replace the pickle in a ploughman's lunch.

500 g / 1 lb ripe, blemish-free tomatoes cored and coarsely chopped
500 g / 1 lb damsons, stones removed, coarsely chopped
200 g / 7 oz sugar
30 ml / 1 fl oz / ⅛ cup freshly squeezed lime juice
75 g / 2 ½ oz freshly grated ginger root
150 g / 5 oz red onion, finely chopped
1 teaspoon ground cumin
½ teaspoon ground cinnamon
¼ teaspoon ground cloves
1 teaspoon fine sea salt
1 jalapeño, seeds and stem removed, minced or grated

In a heavy, medium saucepan, combine all the ingredients and bring to the boil, then reduce to a simmer. Stir occasionally at first, and constantly once the mixture starts to thicken. After 60-90 minutes, it should look jammy and thick. Store in the refrigerator and use within two weeks, or in heat-processed jars for long-term storage.

DAMSON KETCHUP

This recipe comes from Marion Harris Neil's 1914 book, *Canning, Preserving, and Pickling*. Neil's inclusion of seventeen recipes for ketchups was exceptional for the time, according to ketchup historian Andrew F. Smith, since the making of home-made ketchup decreased in the United States as commercially prepared ketchups became widely available. The following is adapted from Smith's reprint of Neil's recipe in *Pure Ketchup: A History of America's National Condiment, with Recipes*.

1 kg / 2 lb damsons
½ teaspoonful salt
125 g / 4 oz granulated sugar

½ teaspoon ground cinnamon
½ teaspoon ground allspice
¼ teaspoon ground cloves
pinch red pepper
250 ml / 8 fl oz / 1 cup water

Wash the damsons, put them into a porcelain-lined saucepan with the water. Simmer until they are perfectly tender, then press them through a sieve or fruit press, rubbing through as much of the skin as possible. Return this to the pan, add the sugar, salt, and spices, and simmer until thick. Bottle and seal.

DAMSON GOCHUJANG BARBECUE SAUCE

This spicy-sweet sauce gets its kick from gochujang, a fermented Korean chili paste. It's delicious on pulled pork or chicken, or swirled into rich broth-based soups. To make ginger juice, press finely grated fresh ginger root against a sieve to extract its juice. Store/serve the finished sauce in a squeeze bottle.

500 g / 1 lb damsons
1 tablespoon high-quality gochujang
50 ml / 1 ¾ fl oz / ¼ cup freshly squeezed lime juice
200 g / 7 oz soft brown sugar
2 tablespoons fresh ginger root juice

In a shallow baking dish, cook damsons at 190 C / 375 F until they soften and release their juices, about 15 minutes. Allow to cool. Drain off the excess juice and set it aside for another use. Remove stones from the softened, cooled damsons. (Be careful not to miss any!) Combine the pulp and skins in a blender with the remaining ingredients. Blend until smooth. Taste and adjust by adding more lime juice, ginger juice, or brown sugar. If the mixture is too runny, simmer over low heat to thicken. Use within two weeks, or freeze for future use.

Spicy Damson Pasta Sauce

Damson purée takes the place of tomato in this silky smooth, gorgeous coloured pasta sauce. To make damson purée, cook damsons over a medium-high heat with a little water until they break down, then rub through a sieve to remove skins and stones.

500 g / 1 lb onions, thinly sliced
25 g / 1 oz fresh garlic, thinly sliced or minced
a few tablespoons butter or olive oil
225 g / 7 ½ oz shop-bought roasted red peppers, drained
150 ml / 5 fl oz / ⅔ cup unsweetened damson purée
2 tablespoons harissa

Cook onions and garlic slowly in butter or olive oil until silky and beginning to caramelize. Blend with remaining ingredients to a smooth, uniform consistency.

Damson Apple Sauces

These beautiful pink apple sauces bring welcome colour to the table. The rosemary variation works well as an accompaniment to meaty mains, while the vanilla bean variation is better suited to the dessert course. Use prepared damson purée from the freezer instead of whole damsons and skip the sieving step for a chunkier apple sauce. If making a large batch, preserve using the water-bath method by pouring into hot, wide-mouth jars. Run a butter knife along the inside of the jar to disperse visible air bubbles before affixing lids. Process in boiling water 15 minutes for small jars and 20 minutes for large jars. Allow jars to rest in the hot water for an additional 5 minutes after removing from heat.

Rosemary Scented Damson Apple Sauce

3 kg / 6 lb apples, peeled, cored, and sliced

500 g / 1 lb damsons
4 tablespoons lemon juice
1 modest handful fresh rosemary sprigs
2 tablespoons maple syrup (or sweetener of choice)
butter for serving

Combine apples, damsons, and lemon juice in a large pot over a medium-low heat. Fold the rosemary sprigs into a compact bundle and enclose in muslin, tying with string to create a sachet. Tuck the sachet among the fruit. Cover and simmer until the apples reduce to form a sauce, stirring periodically; timing depends on the apple varieties used. Remove the rosemary sachet. Rub through a fine sieve to remove stones/skins and create a finer texture. Stir in the maple syrup. Dab the warm sauce with butter before serving.

Vanilla Spiced Damson Apple Sauce

3 kg / 6 lb apples, peeled, cored, and sliced
500 g / 1 lb damsons
4 tablespoons lemon juice
1 whole vanilla bean, split and scraped to loosen seeds
2 tablespoons maple syrup (or sweetener of choice)
1 teaspoon cinnamon or mixed spice
butter (plain or brandied) for serving

Combine the apples, damsons, lemon juice, and vanilla bean seeds and pod in a large pot over medium-low heat. Cover and simmer until the apples reduce to sauce, stirring periodically; timing depends on apple varieties used. Remove the seed pod. Rub through a fine sieve to remove stones/skins and create a finer texture. Stir in the maple syrup and cinnamon. Dab the warm sauce with butter before serving.

Damson Lime Salad Dressing

Serve this zesty Thai-inspired dressing on a salad of butter lettuce, red onion, and chopped coriander topped with grilled sliced beef. Best the day it's made.

100 g / 3 ½ oz damson purée
50 ml / 1 ¾ fl oz / ¼ cup lime juice
50 ml / 1 ¾ fl oz / ¼ cup pomegranate molasses
25 ml / 1 fl oz / ⅛ cup rice wine vinegar
100 ml / 3 ½ fl oz / ½ cup flavourless oil

Blend ingredients thoroughly to emulsify. Serve immediately.

Damson Ginger Sauce

Inspired by a fatless yet creamy rhubarb sauce in Mary Prior's *Rhubarbaria*, this citrusy magenta sauce pairs well with pork and makes an unexpected, vivid accompaniment to salmon.

250 g / 8 oz damsons, stones removed
1 fresh shallot, chopped, or 1 tablespoon freeze-dried shallots
50 ml / 1 ¾ fl oz / ¼ cup orange juice
zest of half a large orange
50 ml / 1 ¾ fl oz / ¼ cup water
1 teaspoon peeled and finely grated fresh ginger root
1-2 tablespoons maple syrup or soft brown sugar (optional)
salt and pepper

Combine all ingredients except syrup in a medium pan. Cook over low heat for 10 minutes. Blend (an immersion blender used right in the pan works great) and adjust sweetness to taste by gradually adding the maple syrup or brown sugar.

“ It is peculiar how important where you are is to the flavour and your enjoyment of a particular drink. If you go to the West Indies and have Planter's Punch or any variation on rum drinks, it's a drink to die for. You go down to Brazil, they make a *caipirinha* and you pestle away at your lime, and you're outside, and it's wonderful. If you come back to London and order these drinks, it doesn't work at all. If you take your damson gin, and you've got a fire going, and you've just had your cheese and a nice meal, you'd sit very happily putting the world to rights and quietly go through quite a lot of damson gin, I suspect. ”

John Cushing, Proprietor, Goldstone Hall Hotel,
Market Drayton, Shropshire

Damson Drinks

Damson Gin Liqueurs

A stroll through the farm shops of damson-growing regions will yield a bounty of damson gins, but these fruity tipples are easily made at home. The practice of steeping damsons in gin likely finds its precursor in earlier gins flavoured with sloes, the fruit of the spine-bearing hedgerow bush also known as blackthorn (*Prunus spinosa*). Fruit infusions in alcohol were common in the seventeenth century, and cookbooks of the time contain numerous recipes for cordial-waters, fruit brandies, ratafias, and shrubs (Seville orange or lemon peel steeped in brandy). Fruit-infused brandies were an appealing option in households that didn't have a still; their preparation was the domain of the lady of the house. These drinks were taken in the banquet course after a large meal as a digestive, or for medicinal purposes, treating problems from indigestion to the common cold.[19] Damson gin carries on this tradition today when used as a cough-soother, or as a warmer-upper on a cold evening.

Damson gin (technically a liqueur due to the added sugar)

was a popular use for damsons in England long before the early twenty-first century craze for craft gins. I've heard tales of cellars filled with undated bottles, ruby red when young and flattening to a tawny shade with age, and elderly neighbours hauling up jars from behind the settee to serve guests. It really is one of the easiest things to do with damsons: the stones are strained out with the fruit prior to bottling, and the preparation consists of three ingredients tumbled into a jar and forgotten. The work is in the waiting. This introduction will help you understand the basics; you can then try one of the recipes that follow (in order from sweetest to driest), or devise your own.

Selecting a Base Spirit

Gin is the classic companion for damsons, as their earthy fruitiness is complemented by the juniper and other botanicals. A neutral spirit, such as vodka or grain alcohol, permits a purer damson flavour. Brandy is an option (apple and brandy being a familiar pairing), but keep in mind that the stronger the distinctiveness of the base spirit, the more diffuse the damson flavour will be. Pre-flavoured spirits are not recommended as they typically possess an artificial taste that will detract from the intense fruit flavour the damsons impart.

Some cookbook authors insist on the finest quality spirits for recipes such as these, but the strong flavour imparted by the damsons, the high sugar content, and the long resting period will mellow the fiercest of cheap spirits. In recipes with shorter infusion times, such as sage-infused gin or jalapeño-infused tequila, the starting quality of the spirits matters; inexpensive gin bottled with damsons and sugar and rested for six months will be surprisingly smooth. Cheap spirits require the investment of patience to pay their dividends.

Any spirit that is 70 proof or higher may be used. Alcohol content will be diluted by the water drawn from the fruit, meaning that a lower proof spirit (such as wine) may not safely preserve the fruit and fully inhibit bacterial growth. Alcohol is a solvent, so the higher the alcohol content, the faster the spirits will draw colour and flavour from the fruit. The added sugar hastens the process by macerating the fruit, so if you decide to reduce the amount of added sugar, you must prolong the resting time. With high-sugar recipes, such as the first one offered below, the resting time may be reduced. The fruit must always be completely covered by the liquid; a few centimetres of spirits above the level of the fruit is the minimum requirement. Fresh fruit tends to float, so weigh it down with a small cup or saucer (depending on your jar) to keep it submerged until it eventually sinks on its own. One occasionally encounters a recipe that instructs to pre-cook the fruit before adding it to the spirits, or infusing spirits with unsweetened fruit and then adding a syrup to sweeten before bottling. Both complicate an otherwise simple process, and neither alternative yields a result as good as the methods outlined below.

Preparing the damsons

Damsons should be clean, dry, and stripped of stalks and leaves. Fruit must be pristine and not overripe. The smallest bruise or trace of rot can spoil the flavour of the batch and introduce bacteria. (You will know this has happened if you open a jar and perceive a sour or rotten odour.) To hasten the process of infusion, the skins of the damsons should be ruptured prior to infusing. There are several options for preparing the damsons after they are cleaned and patted dry:

- For small or very firm damsons, use a small knife to make a deep cut around the horizontal axis of the plum and then around the vertical axis. Cut all the way through to the stone.

- Prick each plum 15-20 times with a sterile needle, a fondue/cocktail fork, cake tester, or other pointy kitchen implement.

- Freeze the damsons, which ruptures the cell membranes, then thaw and use. This is by far the easiest method! I give each thawed damson a little squeeze to split the skin as I drop it in the jar. For large, perfectly ripe damsons, a squeeze without prior freezing may do the job.

SUPPLIES

Large, tightly sealing jars work best (clamp-style Kilner jars are great), but other types of jars may be used. Add up the volume of ingredients for the batch size you're planning beforehand to ensure a large enough jar. I have an inexpensive, gallon size glass jar with a screw-on lid that I use for making fruit liqueurs throughout the year. Every three months, the spirit and the fruit mix inside it changes. In spring, it's rhubarb, in summer, sour cherries, in fall, damsons, and in winter, cranberries. If using a number of small jars instead of one large one, take care to distribute the ingredients evenly. You may wish to combine the final strained liquors from all jars together before bottling to ensure a consistent flavour across the batch. All jars should be spotlessly clean, washed with hot soapy water, rinsed thoroughly, and placed to dry for 10-15 minutes in a 110 C / 230 F oven. The jars must be allowed to cool completely before adding the fruit and spirits. (When making jam, jars should be filled hot; here, the ingredients are room temperature. Always match the jar's temperature to the content's temperature at the time of filling.) A small sauce ladle works well to dip out testing drams if using a narrow mouth jar.

RESTING THE SPIRITS

It is imperative to permit fruit-infused spirits a leisurely resting period in a dark place, at room temperature or cooler. An opaque jar may be left out, but a glass vessel should always be stored away from light. Exposure to light can gradually degrade the quality and the colour of the product. Damson gins kept for long periods will naturally fade from rich ruby to murky burgundy over time. A convenient timeline for damsons is to add the fruits to the spirits at the September harvest time and leave at least until Christmas. Taste-testing can begin earlier if you're curious, but try to wait three months before straining and bottling. After three months, the fruit will have given up its flavour and the liquid will be richly coloured. The longer the spirits rest, the more mellow, ripe, and 'round' the flavours will become. Six months, or even a year, will produce a superior product; a simple recipe for damson gin that appeared in the *Irish Times* in 1929 advised waiting until the next damson season to strain and bottle if the gin was to be at its best.[20] Years ago, I made damson liqueur with inexpensive vodka for the first time, and I tasted it too early. Disappointed, I shoved it back into the cupboard and was not tempted to try it again. A year later, I came across the forgotten bottle and gave it another taste. It was greatly improved. I strained the stones and pulp out, re-bottled it, and then forgot about it again! By year two, when I pulled the bottle out, some remaining sediment had settled to the bottom and the liqueur was beautifully clear. The flavour was exquisite. If you can discipline yourself, you will be rewarded.

When you are satisfied with the intensity of the damson flavour, strain the finished spirits through a muslin-lined sieve or jelly bag to catch small fibres of damson flesh. Decant into bottles washed and dried per the instructions for preparing infusion jars above.

※

The following recipes will work with *Prunus insititia* (damsons or bullaces) as well as *Prunus spinosa* (sloes). Bullaces and sloes may require a bit more sugar. It is tempting to get creative and add spices and other ingredients, but my philosophy is to keep flavours separate and discover affinities at the stage of mixing cocktails. Damsons will predictably pair with cinnamon and star anise, but if these whole spices are left to infuse for months at a time, they may become overpowering. Consider, instead, making batches of simple syrup or bitters flavoured with the desired spices, or infusing higher quality spirits with herbs, whole spices, or chillis over a few days. Producing these separately and mixing to taste with the damson liqueur permits a wider scope for experimentation without risking a whole batch. Damson Simple Syrup and Shrub (also found in this chapter), can add a quick damson flavour to drinks without the months-long wait of liqueurs.

Damson Liqueur #1

The best damson gin liqueur I've ever tasted was a gift from Anne Makin-Taylor of Kendal. Following her mother's method, she combines the ingredients in glass sweetie jars. This liqueur features a high fruit/sugar-to-liquor ratio, making it a soothing remedy for a cough or sore throat. Because it has a high sugar content, this liqueur tastes quite nice after only a week or two, but let it rest longer, as it will only get better. The step of slashing the damson skins may be omitted if the fruit has been previously frozen. For giving, decant the ruby-red elixir into small bottles, cork, and seal beautifully with scarlet wax, as Makin-Taylor does.

2 kg / 4 lb damsons, stray leaves and stems discarded and skins slashed
1-1.5 kg / 2-3 lb sugar (caster sugar dissolves quickest but granulated will do just as well)
70 cl / 1 ¼ pints / 2 ¾ cups of gin

Combine the ingredients in a large glass jar with a tight-fitting lid. Store in a cool, dark cupboard, swishing periodically until the sugar is dissolved, then let stand for at least three months (or longer, see above). Strain the infused spirits to remove the pulp and stones. Repeated strainings through fine muslin will clarify the liquid further, but a bit of sediment at the bottom of the bottle is harmless. After at least one straining, the liqueur may be bottled for gifts or personal use.

DAMSON LIQUEUR #2

Adapt this recipe to the amount of damsons you have by allowing ¼ kilo / 8 oz sugar and 500 ml / ⅞ pint of spirits per kilo / 2 lb of damsons.

> *1.5 kg / 3 lb damsons (washed, dried, stalks removed and skins ruptured)*
> *375 g / 13 oz sugar*
> *1 litre / 1 ¾ pints vodka*

Follow the method for Damson Liqueur #1.

DAMSON LIQUEUR #3

For those with great patience and a desire for a drier tipple, follow the method above using 100 g / 3 ½ oz sugar and 250 g / 8 oz damsons per 500 ml / ⅞ pint of spirits. Rest for at least one year. The damson flavour in this liqueur will be subtle compared to #1 and #2.

DAMSON SHRUBS

Shrubs are sweetened, fruit-infused vinegars that can be mixed with cold water (still or sparkling) to make a refreshing beverage. Throughout the eighteenth century, 'shrub' referred to a brandy or rum steeped with citrus, not a vinegar-based beverage. In the early nineteenth century, 'quick' fruit vinegars consisting of fresh fruit steeped in vinegar and sugar were mixed with water for a restorative drink. Lydia Marie Child was the first to apply the old term, 'shrub,' to these vinegar-based drinks. The name caught on, with subsequent shrub recipes calling for both spirits and vinegar, or just vinegar as a base. Shrub syrups came back into vogue in the early twenty-first century as tart additions to posh craft cocktails. The shrub variations that follow can be served simply in sparkling water, lemonade, or tonic; start with one part shrub syrup to six parts base and increase the shrub to taste. You may wish to experiment with vinegars and sugars other than those indicated. When selecting a vinegar, taste it straight from the spoon first. Even with the addition of fruit and sugar, a harsh, unpleasant vinegar flavour will still come through. Always begin with a vinegar that tastes good on its own. Fresh or frozen damsons may be used.

Spiced Damson Shrub

250 g / 8 oz halved damsons
225 g / 7 ½ oz granulated sugar
250 ml / 8 fl oz / 1 cup apple cider vinegar
3 whole cloves
1 whole allspice
½ a star anise
2.5 cm / 1 in cinnamon stick (Ceylon preferred)

Vanilla Peppercorn Damson Shrub

250 g / 8 oz halved damsons
225 g / 7 ½ oz granulated sugar
250 ml / 8 fl oz / 1 cup decent, moderately aged balsamic vinegar
½ vanilla bean, split and scraped
5 whole peppercorns

Wrap whole spices and/or seeds in a cloth and bash lightly with a rolling pin. Toss with the fruit and sugar in a bowl or jar. Cover. After 2-3 days maceration time at room temperature, add the vinegar. After two weeks (up to a month), strain and bottle for use in drinks, sauces, and salad dressings. Refrigerated, shrubs will stay fresh for well over a year.

Damson Simple Syrup

This simple syrup adds damson flavour to cocktails without the long wait time of damson liqueurs. This recipe keeps the tart flavour of damsons prominent; lemon juice is added to balance the sweetness of the sugar.

500 g / 1 lb damsons
175 g / 6 oz lemon juice
325 g / 11 oz water
500 g / 1 lb granulated sugar

Combine all the ingredients in a medium saucepan and simmer until the damsons are soft. Strain through fine muslin or a jelly bag. Cool and bottle. The syrup will keep for a long time in the refrigerator.

Damson Cordial

Cordials are reduced, sweetened fruit juices bottled for later dilution in anything from plain water to prosecco. The process is similar to making jelly: cook the fruit, strain through a jelly bag, then cook the strained juice with sugar. (The pulp may be used to make a sauce or spread.) By stopping cooking the mixture at a lower temperature, the setting point is not achieved, and the juice does not gel. A ratio of one to two parts cordial in five parts water or sparkling wine should be about right for drinks. Note that, because cordials require such a high ratio of sugar to juice, this recipe retains the fruitiness of the damson but its characteristic astringency will be significantly muted. This cordial tastes generally plummy, but not particularly damson-y.

500 g / 1 lb damsons
600 g / 1 ¼ lb sugar
500 ml / ⅞ pint water

Boil the damsons in the water for 45-50 minutes, until completely soft. Strain the mixture through muslin or a jelly bag, capturing it in a clean pan. If a perfectly clear cordial is desired, refrain from pressing the fruit or squeezing the jelly bag. Add the sugar to the strained liquid over low heat for a further few minutes, until sugar dissolves. Cool thoroughly before bottling. Refrigerate for several months.

Damson Mulled Wine

Damsons add a rich earthiness to this variation on German Glühwein. Make the syrup in advance, later heating gently with the wine and rum to add fast and festive warmth to winter gatherings. This may be the only situation in which I would ever advocate buying inexpensive red wine, because the wonderful fruit and spice flavours (and the sugar) will smooth away imperfections. Received some questionable bottles as gifts? Here's the ideal way to pleasurably 'dispose' of them.

250 g / 8 oz damsons (fresh or previously frozen and thawed)
200 ml / 7 fl oz / 1 cup water
300 g / 10 oz granulated sugar
1 cinnamon stick
1 star anise
12 whole cloves
1 large orange
750 ml / 1 ½ pints / 3 cups red wine
125 ml / 4 fl oz / ½ cup dark rum (optional)

Over a medium heat, combine damsons, water, sugar, and spices. Give each damson a squeeze as you drop it into the pan. Bring to a gentle boil, letting the damsons break down. Pare six wide ribbons of zest from the orange and add to the pan, then add the juice from the orange. Stir occasionally as the mixture continues to reduce, for about 20-25 minutes. If you heat the mixture too fast or let it get too hot, it may reach the gelling point, so keep it to a low simmer until reduced by a third to a half. Cool the thick, syrupy liquid for a few minutes, then strain through a fine sieve to remove stones, skins, and spices. The syrup may be stored at this point for later use.

Refrigerate for use within a few weeks. About 10 minutes before serving, combine the syrup, wine, and rum in a saucepan and heat until just steaming. (Avoid boiling to keep the alcohol at full strength.) Serve in mugs or thermal glass cups, garnished with fresh orange curls or cinnamon sticks.

NOTES

INTRODUCTION
1. Taylor, 5.
2. West, 357.
3. Faust and Surányi, 199.
4. Faust and Surányi, 184.
5. Janick, 293.
6. Faust and Surányi, 190, 193.
7. Mirabelle plums are yellow in colour with 'very slightly sub-acid or sweet' flesh. They are most popular in France, where they are used for preserves and pastries. Hedrick, 39-40.
8. St. Julien produces fruits so similar to damsons that Hedrick suggests the name simply indicates a damson used as rootstock for grafting, rather than one grown for fruit. Its reputation as a reliable stock for *domestica* plums is well-established. Hedrick, 41.
9. Cherry plums are so named for their resemblance to cherries, being small, round and reddish. The trees are small and shrub-like, with glossy leaves and attractive blossoms. Taylor attributes their appeal to their early ripening, in July, before most plums are available. Taylor, 10.
10. Faust and Surányi, 213.
11. Roach, 148.
12. Faust and Surányi, 199
12. Hogg, 257.
14. Hedrick, 195.
15. Taylor, 5.
16. Damson varieties number in double-digits, but only a few warrant discussion. Shoemaker lists more than twenty damson varieties growing at the Ohio Agricultural Experiment Station at Wooster, Ohio. The less significant, or now obscure varieties include Decks Damson (earlier cropping, but fruit prone to splitting and dropping); Finch Damson (purplish-black, abundant, sweet); Free Damson ('mediocre' fruit and light cropping); Frogmore (an English variety originated c.1870, with fruit lacking in flavour and tree lacking in vigour); Kelso (early but irregular cropping, fruit prone to splitting, good flavour, said to have originated when a vagrant gave the seed to an Ohioan named Kelso); Majestic ('better than average' but 'not sufficiently outstanding'); Mount Logan ('inferior' with fair, small fruit and an 'undesirable narrow, upright habit of growth'); Pringle (fruit 'distinctly sour, and unattractive in appearance'); Riley (chance seedling, c.1901, round fruit good for preserves); and Rivers Early (seedling cultivated by Mr Rivers of Sawbridgeworth, England,

early cropping, prone to splitting, sweet and lacking damson flavour).
17. Shoemaker, 20; Taylor, 115.
18. Taylor, 115.
19. Roach, 153.
20. Hogg, 250.
21. Taylor, 71.
22. Cope, 5.
23. Hedrick, 344.
24. Shoemaker, 4.
25. Hedrick, 184.
26. Shoemaker, 4.
27a.Taylor, 114.
27b. Taylor, 63-64
28. Roach, 156.
29. Taylor, 113.
30. Shoemaker, 12.
31. Taylor, 114.
32. Taylor, 71.
33. Roach, 156.
34. Shoemaker, 18.
35. Taylor, 115.
36. Hedrick, 215.
37. Hedrick 39, 214.
38. Taylor, 6.
39. Shoemaker, 21.
40. Taylor, 6.
41. Quoted in Roach, 147.
42. Wilson, C. Anne (ed.), *A Book of Fruits and Flowers*, 43-44.
43. Abercrombie, 99.
44. Taylor, 107.
45. Taylor, 71.
46. Taylor, 108.
47. Hogg, 257.
48. Shoemaker, 12.
49. Taylor, 107.
50. Hedrick, 39.
51. Hogg, 236.
52. Taylor, 60.
53. Taylor, 75.
54. Shoemaker, 4.
55. Hedrick, 35.
56. Nick Dunn, personal conversation, 6 December 2017.

57. *Westmorland Gazette*, 17 December 1938, quoted in Holmes, 44.
58. Holmes, 44.
59. Extracts are used in small enough amounts that it's perfectly safe to use raw kernels as well. Kernels may be roasted prior to soaking if you're hesitant to use them raw.
60. 'Damson stones and vegetables', 16.
61. Woldring, 543.
62. Taylor, 19.
63. Spinescence is a general feature of almost all young Prunus specimens propagated from seed, starting around year three or four. Even for spiny sloes, the presence of spines decreases with age. Woldring, 542
64. Woldring, 547.
65. Woldring, 536.
66. Sue Chantler, personal conversation, 21 November 2017.
67. Henry Mackley, personal conversation, 21 November 2017.
68. Taylor, 36.
69. Horticulture Statistics, 2016.
70. Number of trees today as estimated by Tim Biddlecombe of the Fruits Advisory Services Team and Brogdale Collections. Personal correspondence via Angela Clutton, 29 November 2017.

DAMSONS IN ENGLAND
1. Woldring, 548.
2. Hedrick, 37; Janick, 290.
3. Faust and Surányi, 207.
4. Roach, 145.
5. Woldring, 548.
6. Faust and Surányi, 207-208.
7. Colquhoun, 20.
8. Faust and Surányi, 202.
9. Woldring, 547.
10. Roach, 144.
11. Adamson, xi.
12. Colquhoun, 52.
13. Roach, 146.
14. Woolgar, 109.
15. Roach, 146.
16. Colquhoun, 55.
17. Janick, 271.
18. Quoted in Roach, 147.
19. Roach, 148.

20. Thirsk, 162.
21. Thirsk, 171.
22. Murrell, title page.
23. Swinburne and Mason, 74-75, 79.
24. Moffet, 278.
25. *Westmorland Gazette*, 8 October 1870, quoted in Holmes, 23.
26. Holmes, 23.
27. Allen, 45-46.
28. Holmes, 25-28.
29. *Westmorland Gazette*, 6 July 1918, quoted in Holmes, 38.
30. Taylor, 63-64.
31. Taylor, 65.
32. Hedrick, 38.
33. Hedrick cites the following colloquial names for wild damsons in America, none of which I have ever heard used: 'Wild, Wheat, Spilling, Donkey, Ass, Hog, and Horse plums.' Hedrick, 39.
34. Shoemaker, 1.
35. A., O.R., 427
36. Hedrick, 39.
37. Wilson, E., 258-259.
38. Holmes, 20.
39. *Westmorland Gazette*, 14 October 1867, quoted in Holmes, 3.
40. Anne Wilson, personal conversation, 23 November 2017.
41. Holmes, 37.
42. *Westmorland Gazette*, 5 July 1919, quoted in Holmes, 39-40.
43. Westmorland Damson Association (www.lythdamsons.org.uk).
44. Holmes, 47.
45. Holmes, 51.
46. Westmorland Gazette, 14 October 1922, quoted in Holmes, 41.
47. Anne Wilson, personal conversation, 10 March 2017.
48. Clifford and King, 430-31.
49. Cater and Cater, 58, 70-71
50. Malkin, Judy. personal interview, 23 November 2017.
51. Cater and Cater, 70-71.
52. Personal correspondence, 4 May 2017.
53. Pybus, M., 106-107.
54. Pybus and Dickins, 44-45.
55. Pybus, M., 108. Confirmation of date and menu for the banquet, Peter Ross, Guildhall Library, personal correspondence, 15 February 2018.
56. Menus in the possession of John Cushing.
57. Emma-Kate Lanyon, Shrewsbury Museum & Art Gallery, personal correspondence, 4 September 2017.

58. 'The Corbet Bed Project' booklet. The Corbet Bed Embroiderers' Trust. 2017 and Leila Corbet, personal conversation, 19 November 2017.

59. Ironbridge Gorge Museum Trust. 'Historic Orchard in Coalbrookdale' press release, 3 December 1993. From the papers of John Cushing.

60. Gillian Crumpton, personal conversation, 21 November 2017.

61. Sue Chantler, personal conversation, 21 November 2017.

62. Stephanie Bellows, personal correspondence, 1 December 2017.

63. Woldring, 547.

64. Steve Halton. Personal correspondence, 30 November 2017.

ADVICE FOR GROWING, BUYING AND STORING DAMSONS

1. Nick Dunn, third-generation proprietor of Frank P. Matthews nursery in the West Midlands, was consulted for this section.

2. Loudon, 1027.

3. Cope, 2; Dunn, personal correspondence, 18 December 2017.

4. Dunn, personal conversation, 6 December 2017.

5. Cope, 12.

6. Taylor, 46.

7. Peter Cartmell, 'Bent Banana Disease', Westmorland Damson Association, 1998 (www.lythdamsons.org.uk/bentbanana.rtf).

8. Cope, 25-26.

9. Cope, 44.

10. Hedrick, 38.

11. Shoemaker, 1.

12. Taylor, 60.

13. Taylor, 58-59.

RECIPES

1. Allen, 23-24, 44-45.

2. Taylor, 65.

3. Byron, 246.

4. Levi, 282.

5. Colwin, 172.

6. *Globe and Mail*, 7 October 1941: 9.

7. Holmes, 6.

8. Cope, 10.

9. Simmons, 69.

10. Simmons, 59.

11. Brears, 141.

12. Woodforde, 273.

13. Frere, 37-39.
14. Dawson, 31.
15. Hieatt, 125.
16. Brears, 169-171.
17. Special thanks to Ivan Day for assistance with this section.
18. 'Damson Gin,' 3
19. For more on shrubs, see Michael Dietsch's *Shrubs: An Old-Fashioned Drink for Modern Times*, Countryman Press, 2016.

BIBLIOGRAPHY

A., O.R. 'Damson Plums'. In *Indiana Farmer's Guide* (1918-1922); 22 April 1922, American Periodicals.

Abercrombie, John. *The British Fruit-Gardener*. London: Lockyer Davis, 1779.

Acton, Eliza. *Modern Cookery, in All its Branches*. London: Longman, Brown, Green, and Longmans, 1845.

Adamson, Melitta Weiss. *Food in Medieval Times*. Westport, CT: Greenwood Press, 2004.

Allen, Gary. *Can It!: The Perils and Pleasures of Preserving Foods*. London: Reaktion, 2016.

Barratt, Victoria. *A Taste of Damsons: From Jelly to Gin*. Westmorland Damson Association, 1997

Beeton, Isabella Mary. *Beeton's Book of Household Management*. London: Beeton Publishing, 1861.

Brears, Peter. *Cooking and Dining with the Wordsworths*. Ludlow: Excellent Press, 2011.

Brears, Peter. *Traditional Food in Shropshire*. Ludlow: Excellent Press, 2009.

Byron, May. *Pot-Luck*. London: Hodder & Stoughton, 1915.

Cassell's Dictionary of Cookery. London: Cassell, Petter, Galpin & Co, 1883.

Cater, Colin, and Karen Cater. *Wassailing: Reawakening an Ancient Folk Custom*. Essex: Hedingham Fair, 2013.

Clifford, Sue, and Angela King. *England in Particular*. London: Hodder & Stoughton, 2006.

Colquhoun, Kate. *Taste: The Story of Britain Through Its Cooking*. New York: Bloomsbury, 2007.

Colwin, Laurie. *More Home Cooking*. London: HarperCollins, 1993.

Cope, Eliphas. *A Practical Treatise on Plum Growing*. New Lisbon, OH: The Buckeye State Print, 1888.

Dalgairns, Mrs. *The Practice of Cookery Adapted to the Business of Every Day Life*. Edinburgh: Robert Cadell, 1829.

'Damson Gin.' *Irish Times*, 30 Sept 1929.

'Damson stones and vegetables.' *The Sunday Times*, 22 Aug 2004.

Davidson, Alan. Fruit: *A Connoisseur's Guide and Cookbook*. New York: Simon & Schuster, 1991.

Dawson, Thomas. *The Good Huswifes Jewell*. London, 1596.

Dean, Jenny. 'Dyeing with Damsons.' Website: Jenny Dean's Wild Colour (www.jennydean.co.uk/dyeing-with-damsons).

Dolby, Richard. *The Cook's Dictionary and House-Keeper's Directory*. London: Henry Colburn and Richard Bentley, 1830.

Fairclough, Margaret Alice. *The Ideal Cookery Book*. London: W.R. Howell & Co, 1910.

Faust, Miklos and Dezsö Surányi. 'Origin and Dissemination of Plums.' *Horticultural Reviews*, 23. 1999: 179-231.

Frere, Catherine Frances (ed.). *A Proper Newe Booke of Cokerye*. Cambridge: W. Heffer & Sons, 1913.

Garrett, Theodore Francis (ed.). *The Encyclopaedia of Practical Cookery*. London: Upcott Gill, 1892.

Glasse, Hannah. *The Art of Cookery Made Plain and Easy*. London: W. Strahan et al., 1774.

Globe and Mail (Toronto), 7 October 1941: 9.

Green, Jonathon. *Green's Dictionary of Slang*. London: Chambers Harrap, 2010.

Hedrick, U.P. *The Plums of New York*. Albany, NY: J.B. Lyon Company, 1911.

Hieatt, Constance B., Brenda Hosington, and Sharon Butler. *Pleyn Delit: Medieval Cookery for Modern Cooks*. Toronto: University of Toronto Press, 1996.

Historie of the Knave of Hearts and the Damson Tarts, The. London, c.1868.

Hogg, Robert. *The Fruit Manual*. London: Cottage Gardner Office, 1860.

Holmes, William John Desmond. 'Fruit growing in the Morecambe Bay area with special reference to Damsons.' An unpublished paper submitted for certificate in Social History, Lancaster University, 25 February 2007. A copy is available in Kendal Library.

Horticulture Statistics, from the Department for Environment, Food

& Rural Affairs, 2016.

Hughson, D. *The Family Receipt-Book*. London: W. Pritchard and J. Bysh. 1817.

Janick, Jules. 'The Origins of Fruits, Fruit Growing, and Fruit Breeding.' *Plant Breeding Reviews*, 25 (edited by Jules Janick), John Wiley & Sons, 2005: 255-320.

Josselyn, John. *New England Rarities*. London, Giles Widdowes, 1672.

Levi, Jane. 'Fruit Preserves.' In *The Oxford Companion to Sugar and Sweets*, edited by Darra Goldstein. Oxford University Press, 2015.

Loudon, John Claudius. *An Encyclopaedia of Gardening*. London: Longman, Hurst, Rees, Orme, Brown, and Green, 1824.

Moffet, Lisa. 'Fruits, vegetables, herbs and other plants from the latrine at Dudley Castle in central England, used by the Royalist garrison during the Civil War.' *Review of Palaeobotany and Palynology*, 73, Issue 1-4, 1992: 271-286.

Murrell, John. *A Delight Full Daily Exercise for Ladies and Gentlewomen*. London: printed by Augustine Mathewes for Thomoas Dewe, 1621.

Neil, Marion Harris. *Canning, Preserving, and Pickling*. London: W & R Chambers, 1914.

Pybus, Keith and Gordon Dickins. *Market Drayton: Then & Now*. Market Drayton Town Council. Wern, Shropshire: North Shropshire Printing Co, 1995.

Pybus, Meg. *Under The Buttercross. Market Drayton A Town of Good Food*. Pybus, 1986.

Roach, F.A. *Cultivated Fruits of Britain: Their Origin and History*. Oxford: Basil Blackwell, 1985.

Rundell, M.E. *A New System of Domestic Cookery*. London: John Murray, J. Harding, and A Constable & Co, 1808.

Schreiter, Rick. *The Delicious Plums of King Oscar the Bad*. Harlin Quist, Inc. 1967.

Shoemaker, J.S. 'Fruit Varieties in Ohio, III: Damson Plums'. *Ohio Agricultural Experiment Station Bulletin* #426. Wooster, Ohio. September 1928.

Simmons, Amelia. *American Cookery. Facsimile of the 1796 Edition*, edited by Karen Hess. Bedford, MA: Applewood Books, 1996.

Smith, Andrew F. *Pure Ketchup: A History of America's National Condiment, with Recipes*. University of South Carolina Press, 1996.

Stephens, Brian. 'Damsons & Dyeing.' Unpublished report for English Nature titled 'The Fruit Trade in the Area of Bewdley and the Wyre Forest,' March 2005, excerpted in *Wyre Forest Study Group Review,* 2006, 52-55.

Swinburne, Layinka, and Laura Mason. '"She Came from a Groaning Very Cheerful..." Food in Pregnancy, Childbirth, and Christening Ritual.' In *Food and the Rites of Passage*, edited by Laura Mason. London: Prospect Books, 2002.

Taylor, H. V. *The Plums of England*. Crosby Lockwood & Son, 1949.

Thirsk, Joan. 'Preserving the Fruit and Vegetable Harvest, 1600-1700.' In *The Country House Garden 1600-1950*, edited by C. Anne Wilson. Sutton Publishing and The National Trust. 1998. 162-176.

Thomas, Taffy. *Lakeland Folk Tales for Children*. Stroud: History Press, 2016.

West, Kevin. *Saving the Season*. New York: Knopf, 2013.

Wilson, C. Anne (ed.). *A Book of Fruits and Flowers, first published in 1653 and here reproduced in facsimile with an introduction*. London: Prospect Books, 1984.

Wilson, C. Anne. 'Stillhouses and Stillrooms'. In *The Country House Kitchen 1650-1900: Skills and Equipment for Food Provisioning*, edited by Pamela A. Sambrook and Peter Brears. Alan Sutton Publishing in Association with the National Trust, 1996.

Wilson, Edward M. 'Some Humorous English Folk Tales', Part Three. *Folklore*, 54.1, March 1943.

Woldring, Hendrik. 'On the Origin of Plums: A Study of Sloe, Damson, Cherry Plum, Domestic Plums, and Their Intermediate Forms.' *Palaeohistoria* 39/40, 1997/1998.

Woodforde, James. *The Diary of a Country Parson (1758-1781)*, edited by John Beresford. London: Oxford University Press, 1924.

Woolgar, C.M. *The Culture of Food in England, 1200-1500*. New Haven: Yale University Press, 2016.

ACKNOWLEDGEMENTS

In the course of researching this book I enjoyed fruitful conversations with Shropshire historians Meg and Keith Pybus, nurseryman Nick Dunn, wassailer Judy Malkin, embroiderer Leila Corbet, ranger Nick Hinchliffe, erstwhile Damson Feast host John Cushing, and Slow Food champions Sue Chantler and Catherine Moran. Gillian Crumpton, Alex Logan, and Richard Aldred of Ironbridge Gorge Museum Trust guided me through the national damson collection. Desmond Holmes generously shared his unpublished paper on the history of damson cultivation in the Morecambe bay area, and a number of historical references herein have been gleaned from his extensive research. During my first visit to the Lake District, I had the pleasure of meeting Anne Wilson of Low Farm when she discovered me wandering outside her barn in the Lyth Valley, photographing dormant damson trees one February afternoon. Seeing Anne has been a highlight of every visit I've made to the area since then.

Research assistance of one kind or another was provided by Stephanie Bellows, Tim Biddlecombe, Angela Clutton, Val Ferriman, Steve Halton, Emma-Kate Lanyon, Yannick Lequitte, Henry Mackley, Anne Makin-Taylor, Irma Majer, Juli McLoone, Laura Motta, Peter Ross, Peter Sheratt, Martin Skipper, Jeremy Smith, Taffy Thomas, and members of the Oxford Symposium on Food and Cookery Facebook group. I purchased exceptional damsons for recipe development and testing at Marker-Miller Orchards of Winchester, Virginia.

I have had the great honour of consulting with Janice Bluestein Longone, benefactor of the Longone Culinary Archive at the University of Michigan, on a number of projects. Jan's generosity and depth of knowledge are legendary. When I mentioned to her in 2015 that I'd be pursuing my damson project, she rapidly produced a copy of U.P. Hedrick's *The Plums of New York*, photocopied a few pages for me, and my bibliography was launched. Culinary historian Ivan Day generously assisted me in tracing the precedents of damson gins and cheeses, and drew my attention to Joseph Bell's 1817 recipe for damson ice cream and Theodore Garrett's 1895 recipe for damson knots.

Catheryn Kilgarriff, English Kitchen series editor at Prospect Books, afforded me the opportunity to write a book I was yearning to write, and guided the project to completion. Brendan King provided meticulous editing and fact-checking. Photo editor Sharon Hume and graphic designer Jackie Vanderzwaag created a gorgeous book cover. To all, I owe my gratitude.

Bradley Taylor shares my love of English heritage and landscape, and is always ready to offer an encouraging word when one needs it most. Lucy Long taught a graduate seminar in food studies that set the course for my future work in ways I could not yet imagine. My great-uncle Wayne Conrad and great-aunt Betty Horetsky shared memories of their grandmother's jam-making, and great-aunt Carol Conrad recalled 'those funny little plums' that grew in the family's backyard.

Helen Platt has been my agent on the ground, following up leads, chauffeuring me to meetings, and hosting me during research trips. Without Helen's friendship and hospitality, this book may have never materialized. Helen has been to me, as Mrs. Beeton described the damson, 'invaluable.' Lastly, I am grateful for the wholehearted support of Laura, Roy, and Dashiell. They share my love of damsons, an ancient fruit that will always have a place of honour on our family's table.

INDEX

All recipes are listed alphabetically under RECIPES.